Living in the Shadow of a Hell Ship

The Survival Story of U.S. Marine George Burlage, a WWII Prisoner-of-War of the Japanese

Georgianne Burlage, editor

Number 18 in the North Texas Military Biography and Memoir Series

University of North Texas Press

Denton, Texas

10 9 8 7 6 5 4 3 2 1

Permissions:
University of North Texas Press
1155 Union Circle #311336
Denton, TX 76203-5017

The paper used in this book meets the minimum requirements of the American National Standard for Permanence of Paper for Printed Library Materials, z39.48.1984. Binding materials have been chosen for durability.

Library of Congress Cataloging-in-Publication Data

Names: Burlage, George, 1918-2008, author. | Burlage, Georgianne, 1955- editor.
Title: Living in the shadow of a hell ship : the survival story of U.S. Marine George Burlage, a WWII prisoner-of-war of the Japanese / edited by Georgianne Burlage.
Other titles: North Texas military biography and memoir series ; no. 18.
Description: Denton, Texas : University of North Texas Press, [2020] |
Series: North Texas military biography and memoir series ; Number 18 |
Includes bibliographical references and index. | Summary: "Book is a daughter's story of her father's experience as a Japanese POW in World War II. She has written an intro and assembled his notes and memoir of his experiences"-- Provided by publisher.
Identifiers: LCCN 2020018763 | ISBN 9781574418088 (cloth) | ISBN 9781574418170 (ebook)
Subjects: LCSH: Burlage, George, 1918-2008. | United States. Marine Corps. Marine Regiment, 4th--Biography. | World War, 1939-1945--Prisoners and prisons, Japanese. | Prisoners of war--Philippines--Biography. | Prisoners of war--United States--Biography. | Prisoners of war--Transportation--Pacific Ocean--History--20th century. | Prison hulks--Japan--History--20th century. | World War, 1939-1945--Campaigns--Philippines--Corregidor Island--Biography. | World War, 1939-1945--Personal narratives, American. | LCGFT: Autobiographies.
Classification: LCC D805.J3 B833 2020 | DDC 940.54/7252092 [B]--dc23
LC record available at https://lccn.loc.gov/2020018763

Number 18 in the North Texas Military Biography and Memoir Series

The electronic edition of this book was made possible by the support of the Vick Family Foundation.

To George Burlage –He and many of his generation refused to give up when faced with defeat. Our debt to them can never be repaid.
To Rachel Burlage and Leah Burlage – Their grandfather often said that he fought for the right to have a future. They continue their grandfather's legacy.

Table of Contents

List of Illustrations

Editor's Introduction

The Recruiter Didn't Mention This Possibility

When he was captured, he had sworn to survive. No one would rob him of his future. Although he was a prisoner-of-war of the Japanese, he wasn't giving up. Survival wouldn't be easy, and there were times when staying alive was more luck than strategy.

George Burlage, my father, was captured on May 6, 1942, when the fortress island of Corregidor in the Philippines was surrendered to the Imperial Japanese Army. He survived beatings, starvation, torture, hard labor, a stint as a miner in the mountains of Northern Japan, and thirty-eight days in the hold of a hell ship. He was part of the estimated 60 percent of POWs who survived (Michno 2001).

Why was the death rate among Allied prisoners of the Japanese so high? One reason is cultural. The Code of Bushido, which was emphasized in Japanese military training, stated "it (was) shameful to themselves not to die (in battle)... their shame was the same upon their parents, their family, their house." The greatest honor was to die for the Emperor

(Flanagan 2016). The Japanese believed in the warning "Do not survive the dishonor of capture" (Davis 1994).

There was also a feeling of superiority over Western people. General Hideki Tojo, the Japanese war lord and wartime leader, once commented that white men could go to hell and that the Japanese would send them (Davis 1994). He also instructed POW camp commandants not to worry about humanitarian treatment of their prisoners (Davis 1994).

Throughout history, prisoners-of-war were subjected to extreme consequences like slavery or execution. The objective of taking soldiers as prisoners was to prevent them from returning to their units (Lord Russell of Liverpool 2002). The views about prisoners-of-war changed in the twentieth century with rules about treatment. Meetings at the Hague Convention in 1907 and at the Geneva Accords in 1929 outlined humane treatment including providing adequate housing and food for POWs. Japan had signed these, but the government never ratified the updates (Brady 2003). One American prisoner-of-war later told of when he was captured, he told his interrogator that according to the Geneva Convention, he only had to share his name, rank, and serial number. His interrogator answered that he knew nothing about the Geneva Convention. "We're fighting a war. Don't you know that?" he said. "I can kill you...and no one will ever know I did it." (Brady 2003)

Western thought included the concept that surrender is not sinful if the situation is hopeless. For example, the Corregidor forces were surrendered because they had literally run out of food and ammunition. However, the Japanese philosophy was that any soldier who surrenders forfeits any humane treatment (Lord Russell of Liverpool 2002). General Tojo justified the harsh treatment of their prisoners, generalizing that "in Japan, we have our own ideology concerning prisoners-of-war which naturally would make their treatment different from that in Europe and in America" (Lord Russell of Liverpool 2002). The Japanese believed that there was no honor for prisoners-of-war. They were astonished when the captured Americans requested that their parents be notified of their status. They were sure that the families would be humiliated by their captured sons, brothers, and husbands (Brady 2003).

Japanese historian Ikuhiko Hata described the Bushido culture as "At the heart of the matter lay their (the Japanese military) belief that their own troops on being prisoner should forfeit all human rights. Inevitably, this attitude was applied with equal vigor towards enemy POWs." (Brady 2003)

Burlage witnessed his fellow POWs being shot, bayoneted, forced on marches, beheaded, drowned, and tortured. He watched men enduring the "sun treatment," a special brand of treatment where the prisoner was forced to spend hours in the brutal heat (sometimes in a special box constructed for this purpose) with no water. This usually resulted in heat stroke. A guard at Las Pinas, George's last Philippine camp, specialized in the special torture of putting a water hose in a prisoner's mouth, filling him with water, then jumping on the prisoner's stomach as a punishment. Escape attempts resulted in a trip to Manila for "trial," followed by execution. He was entombed in the bottom of a hell ship for more than a month, fighting to live in the midst of madness.

Why was George Burlage in the Philippines on December 8, 1941? All he wanted was money to finish college. After graduating from junior college, there were no funds for him to continue his education, so joining the Marines seemed like a good idea and perhaps an adventure. The adventure that George Burlage endured, though, was not in his plans nor could have been imagined.

Burlage was officially sworn in as a United States Marine on September 1, 1939. Hitler's invasion of Poland and the beginning of World War II in Europe seemed very far away from San Diego, California, where he was in boot camp. He was sure that he would be sent to Asia with the Fourth Marines and although Japan had invaded China a few years earlier, Americans weren't worried about a war either there or in Europe. The United States had already participated in one world war, and the world fell apart afterwards. Few Americans wanted to get involved in another war.

He was right about his destination. Soon after graduation from boot camp, Burlage was sent to Cavite in the Philippines, one of many American bases that were in the vicinity of Manila. Life was good. He served as a military policeman, and the biggest problems he encountered were drunk Marines getting into fights. There was cold San Miguel beer to enjoy and plenty of down time. Military life was good.

When his two years in the Philippines were ending in early December 1941, Burlage's possessions were packed, and he had moved out of his barracks and was waiting for transport back to the United States where he would complete his four-year enlistment. His post-Marines plans were to enroll at Fresno State. He wanted to be a history teacher. However, Japan had other plans.

When Pearl Harbor was attacked on December 7, 1941, it was already December 8 in the Philippines. The Japanese wasted no time in bombing the Philippines and other Western-controlled areas in Asia. The Allied forces were not prepared. They had World War I-era antiaircraft guns whose range was not high enough for the new Japanese bombers. Ammunition was low. The forces knew that they had to have reinforcements to have even a chance to survive.

He was captured at Corregidor on May 6, 1942, a date that was always embedded in his memory until he passed away at age ninety. His ATM PIN was 5642 in honor of what he always referred to as "the worst day of my life." During the next forty months, George Burlage would endure starvation, beatings, slave labor, and a thirty-eight -day hell ship voyage in almost total darkness.

When he was captured, George swore that he would survive his captivity, and he did. His postwar life was successful and content, but it was obvious that he had survived experiences that few have endured. During the last days of his life, many of these long-withheld emotions surfaced, and he mentally relived the hell of being a prisoner-of-war. He clawed the air and yelled, and he was restrained in his hospital bed with his hands covered in protective mittens.

Surfaced Memories

Not too long after midnight on November 30, 2008, my phone rang. The intensive care nurse from the hospital where George Burlage, my dad, was recovering from hernia surgery asked me to come immediately. My ninety-year-old father was in cardiac arrest.

When I arrived at the hospital, the nurse told me that my dad had been hallucinating. She said that he was yelling statements like, "You can't do this to us. We'll die down here," "Let us out! No! No! No!" "Get away from me!" and "Don't trap us down here." In his last moments on earth, George Burlage was reliving his worst moments of his long life: being trapped in the hold of the ship with a thousand men, fighting to stay alive, stuffed in an area with a thousand men, all fighting to stay alive in total, suffocating darkness.

Except for forty months, George Burlage had an exceptional life. He was educated, respected, and successful, and his family adored him. His only regret, he would say, was that my mother died too young and he had to experience long years of being a widower. He often remarked that he never forgave his Japanese captors but that he let his anger go. If he didn't do so, he was allowing his POW experiences too much power over his life. I even bought a Mazda, and he said he was "over it" although later, while looking at my Mazda and my daughter's Volkswagen side-by-side in the garage, he did observe, "Two-thirds of the Axis in my garage." Still, his last thoughts were of being in the hold of the *Hokusen Maru*, also known as the "Horror Maru" and the "Benjo Maru." What had happened in that hold?

Statistics tell one side of what happened, but they don't describe the personal horrors of the hell ships. I doubt if I will ever know the entirety of what my dad experienced even though I have read his personal accounts and his oral history. However, this is what I do know: the hell ships survivors experienced a human form of hell on earth.

After he retired, George annually spoke to my high school history classes about his war experience and wrote numerous articles and gave many speeches about what he endured. As the years progressed, his presentations' content intensified, and I know that my students' respect for this aging veteran was sincere. He would start his talks with Corregidor and the circumstances of his capture and then share stories of the POWs' sabotage efforts such as destroying equipment, constructing uneven runways, stealing beer, and breaking arms. He told the students that much of the POW experience was tolerable and that the main survival tip was to be "one step ahead" of his captors.

"Then there was a situation none of us could anticipate," he would state, "and that was the hell ships." He joked a bit, telling that when he first saw the ships lined at the Manila pier, he thought, "Well, that won't be so bad. We'll be in cabins, or at the very least, we'll be on the deck." Then he realized that the prisoners were going to be stacked back-to-breast in the hold of a cargo ship that reeked of horse manure. He shared the panic that he felt when the doors to the hold were slammed shut and winched down, preventing any possibility of escape and blocking out light. When the men were plunged into total darkness, the screams and the pleas began. Many became crazed, stepping on other prisoners and killing one another. He would spare no description of the horror, the hell, that he lived through. When he described men being so crazed from thirst that they would attack other men, biting throats in the pursuit of moisture, students' wincing and gasping could be heard.

He told about his friend offering him morphine and attempting to persuade George to kill himself to escape the horror. In his typical matter-of-fact way, my dad responded, "No, thanks. I'll stick around and see what happens." He made this decision while listening to American attacks on nearby hell ships.

The students realized that they were listening to a heroic man who wouldn't claim heroism. "My country needed me," he always said, "and I served my country."

When I was younger, I didn't realize that my dad's idiosyncrasies were caused by his hell ship experiences. Several times, we made family road trips between Texas and California, and I would beg to stop at New Mexico's Carlsbad Caverns. My answer always came from my mother —"Your father doesn't like caves" —with no explanation. He avoided elevators when possible. His offices always had windows. We often had to close blinds and curtains in our home because my dad wouldn't. He spent as much time as he could outdoors and loved landscaping. We rarely ate rice because he identified it with his POW days. Later, I learned that when he was assigned to Navy ships after World War II, he would sleep on the open deck or in a deck-top location, not below with the other men. His colleagues knew why.

The most lasting effect of those thirty-eight days in the hold of the *Hokusen Maru,* though, was George Burlage's generosity. He was truly grateful that he had survived, and his gratitude was evident through his altruism. He was successful, and he shared. Every year, he purchased blankets for our city's homeless shelters in honor of his fellow POWs who froze to death in the Japanese mines. He gave his time and his financial contributions to our community's veteran causes. He was active in his church, and he established endowments at the University of North Texas (his alma mater) and the Denton (Texas) Public Schools Foundation. He was selfless, and he was thankful to be able to serve and to give back.

His most selfless act was to help raise his granddaughters after my divorce. My parents provided us with a home, and my dad paid for my daughters' college educations. He also cared for my mothers' parents in their declining years. However, these qualities resulted from his experiences of surviving forty months behind barbed wire.

How did he survive?

CHOOSING TO SURVIVE

Gavan Davis, writing in his book *Prisoners of the Japanese—POWs of World War II in the Pacific* makes these assertions:

1. Nothing close to respect for the enemy or respect were present in the POW camps in the Pacific Theater in World War II.
2. The Japanese believed that white men who allowed themselves to be captured where despicable.
3. The Japanese were not directly genocidal, but their treatment of their prisoners caused a high rate of death. Torture, beheading, beating, starvation, even keeping Red Cross packages from their prisoners were regular events. The men who survived could only look forward to more hard work and mistreatment.
4. Almost all the prisoners had been captured at the beginning of World War II and spent the war in POW camps. Also, more than Americans were in the camps. Australian, Dutch, and British military were also prisoners (Davis 1994).

The prisoners who survived had to decide when the standard belief that a person must help his fellow man was not applicable. Starvation was often the deciding factor. Men like Burlage traded their cigarette rations for additional food from fellow POWs. He would often talk about how he caused the deaths of several fellow POWs with the unapologetic explanation, "If a person would rather smoke than eat, it's his decision. I didn't steal their rations. They gave them to me." The men who survived also witnessed friends die, often in brutal ways. When the war was over, the camp survivors struggled with their experiences and choices back in the world. The will to live is strong, but it can come with a steep price.

Davis also maintained that there were common scenarios in the POW camps:

1. Trading food for tobacco
2. Self-mutilation to avoid work like self-inflicted wounds and arm breaking

3. Giving up and willing oneself to die
4. Totally relying on God to save oneself
5. Having to kill a fellow prisoner or be killed (for example, in the hell ships) (Davis 1994).

The prisoners-of-war who survived had to live with what they experienced and what they witnessed. They had to learn to live with their experiences, or it could destroy them (Davis 1994).

But George Burlage survived. He participated in petty sabotage like stealing guards' beer, taking spark plugs out of trucks, mixing concrete incorrectly, knocking over the survey sticks at the airfield construction sites, playing tricks on guards, and pulling the pins out of the mine carts that resulted in runaway carts. He came close to crossing the line with his arm-breaking "career," but the Americans' return to the Philippines saved him.

The men who survived the Japanese camps were tough and, some would claim, lucky. Burlage often commented that he had to predict his guards' next moves and to plan ahead. He volunteered for work details so that he could forage for food. He learned enough Japanese to listen for information from the guards. He was successful in his attempt to leave Cabanatuan, a huge prisoner camp that was teeming with disease and starvation, and he managed to obtain a transfer from Palawan fifteen months before the massacre. He traded his cigarette rations for food. His philosophy was that every day he survived was a day closer to liberation.

George Burlage survived while so many did not. He left his years of captivity with minimal physical damage except for conditions caused by malnutrition. He did carry obvious mental scars, though—survivor's guilt and Post Traumatic Stress Syndrome (PTSD).

PTSD was not defined until 1980 when the condition was included in the Diagnostic and Statistical Manual of Mental Disorders (DSM-11) (PTSD: National Center for PTSD n.d.). The determination was made that a traumatic event can result in emotional problems and that these problems are not caused by weakness or neurosis.

In the fall of 2019, I participated in the Japanese-sponsored POW Friendship trip. A group of Japanese POW researchers arranged a forum to discuss prisoner-of-war issues with us descendants. While waiting to share my views and experiences, I listened to the other participants' stories about their fathers. They told stories that deeply moved me:

1. One woman remembered an occasion when she startled her father. He jumped out of his chair, lunged at his daughter, and began to choke her. He was experiencing a flashback from the camps.
2. A man told that his father had a quick temper and that beating his children was his response to every situation.
3. Another woman shared that when her father returned home, he vowed to never leave again. He never did.
4. Others told of reactions to fireworks and loud noises. One father always slept on the floor.

My father was very quiet, almost shy. He had a sly sense of humor and was very observant. He was not violent and never laid a hand on either my mother or me. He detested hunting, and he would not allow it on his farm saying, "If you had ever been hunted by the enemy in battle, you wouldn't kill innocent animals." We never had firearms in our home. He was very generous, which I attributed to survivors' guilt. He was so grateful that he was alive.

He and I had deep discussions about his experiences after I was an adult. He often wondered why he survived a situation where more than 40 percent of his fellow POWs died. What made him try to leave Palawan where later, he lost so many friends? Why was he sent to Corregidor, avoiding the fate of those who were in the Bataan Death March? He always believed that his vow to survive the war was why he made it through forty months of hell. George's PTSD was largely a result of his long hell ship voyage, which resulted in lifelong problems. He didn't like to be in a crowd. He never sat with his back to a door, and he always located the exit wherever he was. Claustrophobia was a constant issue although being in planes didn't bother him. He would keep blinds and curtains open even after dark, and rooms had to have windows.

George wondered why his hell ship was spared when so many weren't. 10,800 prisoners out of 50,000 died on hell ship voyages. One-third of the Allied prisoners who died during captivity were killed by American bombings and submarines during hell ship voyages (Center of Military History 1989).

He was saved from certain execution because the Americans did not invade Japan. An execution date had been set for the fall of 1945. The goal was to "prevent prisoners of war from falling into enemy hands" (Davis 1994).

Many Fourth Marines never let go of the feeling of abandonment. It is well known that General Douglas MacArthur departed from Corregidor before the surrenders of Bataan and Corregidor, leaving behind thousands of men and women who were doomed to be prisoners-of-war. My dad wrote in his memoirs, "It was like seeing a captain leave his sinking ship. Almost half of the Fourth Marines did not survive the war." The Fourth Marines' surrender was the first time an entire Marine regiment had surrendered (Corregidor.og/usmc n.d.). General "Skinny" Wainwright had defied General MacArthur's order, sent from Australia where he had settled after leaving Corregidor, to fight to the death. In his telegram to President Roosevelt to inform him of the surrender, Wainwright wrote, "With broken heart and head bowed in sadness but not in shame... I must arrange terms for our surrender. My troops and I have accomplished everything that is humanly possible" (Center of Military History 1989). At the war's end, MacArthur excluded the Fourth Marines from a recommendation that the Corregidor defenders receive a presidential unit citation. His reason? He said that Marines "had enough glory in World War I" (Center of Military History 1989).

George Burlage was asked probably hundreds of times how he survived prison camp. His answer was always the same. "I swore when I was captured that I would survive. I made good choices and planned ahead," he would explain. "Even when on that hell ship, I analyzed the situation. I stayed by myself as much as I could, away from the really crazed men. I watched a man trying to dig a hole in the hull because there was water 'on the other side.' I decided how I would escape if the ship were hit. I was always thinking of what could happen next."

Then he would add, "I survived and have had a great life. However, those who didn't make it, my friends on Corregidor and at Palawan are always on my mind." In a speech in 1984 to honor POW Remembrance Day, Burlage admitted, "How did I survive? I really have no idea."

Many former POWs adopted the philosophy "We can forgive, but we can't forget" (Corregidor.og/usmc n.d.). The Fourth Marines adopted the motto "Surrendered, yes. Defeated, no." Both these statements summarize George Burlage. He never forgot the past, but his prisoner-of-war experiences did not defeat him. Luck did play a part, but his determination to survive and to have a future made the difference.

THE MARINE MYSTIQUE

When George Burlage was accepted into the Marine Corps, there were 16,000 Marines in the entire military. The Corps had a mystique that was boosted by the image of the "China Marines" who guarded Americans and American property in that country. They were known as the "First to Fight" Corps. The Fourth Marines had been organized in 1914 and were soon deployed to the Dominican Republic for ten years as a peacekeeping force (www.3rdmardiv.mil) and later began its service in Shanghai and other important Chinese cities in 1927. When World War II was threatening to involve the United States, the regiment was sent to the Philippines in early December 1941 to protect naval stations like Olongapo and Cavite. (www.ibiblio.org) The Fourth Marines were combined with the Marines at these navy yards, men like George Burlage. These Marines and a few smaller units were sent to Bataan in late December 1941 and a few weeks later crossed the short distance to Corregidor to set up beach defenses.

Corregidor's unofficial newspaper, *Navy Evening Gopher*, included "The Corregidor Marines' Hymn" in an edition:

From the holes of Mariveles

To the shores of Cavite

We watch the Nippon bombers

On the land as on the sea.

First to jump for hole and tunnel

And to keep our skivvies clean,

We are proud to claim the title

Of Corregidor Marines.

Our drawers unfurled to every breeze

From dawn to setting sun

We have ducked in every hole and ditch

Where we could quickly run

In the holes of far off hilltops

And in gloomy deep ravines

You will find us always in a hole—

The Corregidor Marines.

Here's holes for you and for our Corps

Which we have dug in dirt

In many a strife we've jumped for life

And damn near lost our shirts

If the Army and the Navy

Ever look out Tunnel Queens

They will find that they are guarded

By Corregidor Marines.

(Gordon 2011)

When Corregidor fell in May 1942, the Fourth Marines ceased to exist. Approximately 2,270 Marines were captured at Corregidor; 268 of these men died in prisoner-of-war camps or on the sea in a hell ship, and 250 are still listed as missing-in-action and presumed dead (ibiblio.org). The Fourth Marines were reactivated in 1944 and fought in Guadalcanal and participated in the island-hopping battles. When the war ended, 1750 Fourth Marines were liberated after serving practically the entire conflict in prison camps.

The surrender of the Fourth Marines at Corregidor was not only a part of the largest surrender (combined with Bataan) in American history but also the example of the only regiment in Marine history to capitulate. The regimental colors were burned as one colonel lamented, "I had to be the first Marine officer ever to surrender a regiment." (Miller 1997)

The first Marines captured in World War II were on Wake Island and Guam. They soon were introduced to the Japanese attitude toward prisoners-of-war. The Japanese believed that POWs were cowards and treated them as inferior. Many of the prisoners were eventually shipped to China and Japan to be slave laborers, and one hundred civilian workers on Wake Island were executed. Other Marine prisoners-of-war were survivors of the sinking of the *USS Houston*. Many of these men wound up working on the Burma-Thailand Railway.

One Size does Not Fit All POWs

The Marines and others who were surrendered to the Japanese probably expected humane treatment from their captors. The statistics indicate otherwise as survival rates of the prisoners were between 50 to 60 percent

(Gordon 2011). The Japanese were fighting for an Asia for Asians concept and to eradicate "the source of evil." Hirohito perceived this war as a war between the yellow and white races, a war where the white leaders greatly underestimated their enemy (MacArthur 2005). Before leaving to fight, Japanese troops were given an anti-West pamphlet, "Just Read This, and the War Is Won." The manual described Westerners as "very effeminate and very cowardly... (with) an intense dislike of fighting in rain or mist or at night..." (MacArthur 2005). The Allied POWs were told, "You have no property. You gave up everything when you surrendered. You do not even own the air in your bodies... You are the slaves of the Japanese." (www.biblio.org) Many guards were sadistic, randomly beating and flogging the prisoners for no reason other than to demonstrate to the world the true worth of Japanese manhood." Their only purpose to exist was to do slave labor for the Japanese (MacArthur 2005).

There were several types of POW camps in the Pacific area that held an estimated 140,000 prisoners of war from Australia, Britain, the Netherlands, and the United States along with a few other nations. In addition, the Japanese held 135,000 civilians—Westerners who lived in the East Indies, the Philippines, French Indochina, and other countries occupied by the Japanese. The estimated more than 700 camps of all sizes were widespread—China, Burma, Formosa, Japan, Java, Malaya, Manchuria, the Philippines, and Thailand. It was not uncommon for prisoners to be transferred to different camps, as slave labor was vital of the Japanese war effort (MacArthur 2005).

The everyday life of a prisoner-of-war was dull and uneventful with the same daily routine of working from dawn to dusk. Most of the camps were in isolated areas, and the guards' goal was not just to supervise but also to break spirits and morale. Types of slave labor included constructing airfields, working as stevedores and on rubber plantations, building railroads, refining oil, building dams, mining, and farming. All of this was for Japan's benefit (MacArthur 2005; www.ibiblio.org). The breakdown of the main nationalities in the camps was—

1. Americans—36,260 military internees—38 percent death rate
2. Australians—21,000 military internees—39 percent death rate
3. British—50,000 military internees—25 percent death rate
4. Indians—25,000 military internees—no information on death rate
5. Dutch—42,000 military internees—15 percent death rate/100,000 civilian internees—25 percent death rate

The various nationalities represented in the camps had distinctive traits. The British were known to be very class conscious with the officers very much in charge. Australian POWs were clever at tricking their captors, and the Americans enjoyed scheming and organizing Mafia-like groups that controlled camp life. The Americans were also characterized by their feelings of superiority and their ignorance about other countries. Both the Americans and the Australians considered the British as arrogant, inflexible, and serious rule followers (MacArthur 2005).

Most British were more cooperative and valued relationships with the Japanese. American prisoners, though, enjoyed minor sabotage against their captors. Some examples were draining gasoline drums and refilling them with water, resulting in damaged planes, and throwing sand in moving machinery to ruin their parts. American stevedores unloaded ships slowly and overloaded cargo nets so that they would burst while suspended over a ship (www.ibiblio.org).

Degradation of POWs

By summer 1942, the Japanese Empire spread four thousand miles across Asia and included five time zones. The Allies had sealed the doom for their troops in the Far East by putting any reinforcements on the proverbial back burner while concentrating on defeating the Fascists in Europe. The situation in Asia, including the fate of the prisoners, was not a priority. The reinforcements that General MacArthur was promising his men just didn't exist (MacArthur 2005).

General Homma answered General King's question about fair treatment of the surrendered troops at Bataan by asserting, "We are not barbarians." However, General Homma's attitude towards the captured men was brutal. The prisoners were frequently reminded that they were alive only "by the grace of the Emperor," and their debt was to work for Japan. The captors were not compassionate or gentle. Existence was in doubt, and lives were at the mercy of the guards. The treatment of the prisoners in the Bataan Death March was an indication of their future. In addition to being marched sixty miles in the Filipino heat with little food, rest, or water, prisoners were searched for valuables, killed if discovered with Japanese items or currency, and were not allowed to have canteens. Those men who stumbled or hesitated on the March were killed. Those who made it to Camp O'Donnell were weak and unwell. During the first few months at the camp, 2,000 Death March survivors died from disease, malnutrition, and mistreatment (www.ibiblio.org). An average of forty to fifty prisoners died every day at the Cabanatuan camp until January 1943.

POW forced labor included anything and anywhere that the Japanese needed for their war effort. There were a few successful escape attempts, but most of the prisoners knew that it was probably futile. The inability of the Allied prisoners to "blend in" with the native population and the Japanese promise to kill prisoners in retaliation for an escape prevented many attempts. If there were a successful attempt like the one at Davao on the island of Mindanao in April 1943, Filipino guerrillas provided shelter and help (Gordon 2011). The POWs who escaped from Davao eventually traveled to Washington, D.C., to share with government officials about the horrors and mistreatment in the prison camps. When the American media finally gained permission to share these stories, the public was justifiably outraged, but no military attempts were planned to rescue prisoners (www.ibiblio.org).

The Burma-Thailand Railway was nicknamed "The Railway of Death" (MacArthur 2005). The Japanese decided in May 1942 that a secure rail line was needed and set a deadline of one year for completion. The railroad would include 688 bridges, blasting through rock, and using simple tools like knives, shovels, and picks. Some workers were permanently blinded by the glare of the clay ground and lack of vitamins. One POW who was a railway worker observed, "Nowhere in the world used sadism as efficient as in the Japanese army." (MacArthur 2005) Every form of cruelty was used by the guards—beating, kicking, kneeling on bamboo, being placed in the hotbox and confined in the sun, solitary confinement, and random brutal punishments. The prisoners also had to fight mosquitoes, lice, bedbugs, dysentery, malaria, beriberi, and cholera. The 258-mile Burma-Thailand Railway was completed on October 25, 1943. The Japanese had met their goal at the cost of 90,000 civilian workers and 12,000 Allied prisoners-of-war out of a slave labor workforce of more than 185,000 (MacArthur 2005).

As the American forces grew closer to the Japanese possessions, the Japanese Imperial Forces decided to transfer the "healthy" prisoners (any who could walk) to Japan to be used as slave laborers in their failing war efforts. An estimated 20,000 POWs died aboard these hell ships, killed by friendly fire. The POWs were stuffed in the holds of unmarked Japanese ships, and the convoys were targets for Allied bombers and submarines that unknowingly killed their own countrymen. The worst months for these voyages was from October to January 1945 when the Allied forces were advancing on the Philippines (Gordon 2011). 184 Fourth Marines were killed aboard hell ships (www.biblio.org).

The survivors of the hell ships worked for Japanese industrial giants. At the Fukoaka Camp 17 on the Japanese island of Kyusha, Americans and Australians worked in the coal mine. The British were assigned to the zinc foundry, and the Dutch worked in the coal stalls, loading coal on ships (MacArthur 2005). At the Wakayana Camp, the copper mines were so hot that work periods had to be shortened. The winter of 1945 was so cold that temperatures fell to minus twenty degrees Fahrenheit. The guards would not allow the workers to wear coats (MacArthur 2005). Safety was not a concern. A copper mine in Taiwan had a death rate of

80 percent. Out of the original 524 men who were sent there, eighty-nine survived. A few prisoners who were assigned to work as welders were blinded because the guards would not supply goggles to them.

The worst camp was Haruku in what is now Indonesia. The Allied POWs, the large majority being Australian and Dutch, were forced to build an airstrip that would be used for strikes against Australia. The working conditions were brutal, and the tools were chisels and hammers. The POWs injured their feet laboring barefoot on the coral surface, causing infections. Pellagra, scurvy, beriberi, skin ulcers, and blindness were results of malnutrition and inhumane labor. When a prisoner warned a camp commandant about the increasing disease and injuries, the prisoner was told "Nice when dead." Soon, the prisoners nicknamed the two head guards "Slime" and "Blood" after dysentery symptoms (MacArthur 2005). One-half of the Haruku POWs died in the camp or on hell ships. "Slime" and "Blood" were sentenced to death in the Singapore War Crimes after the war ended (MacArthur 2005).

Surviving the Unimaginable

When the men were captured and Western civilians in the Japanese-occupied areas were placed in internment camps, four categories of prisoners-of-war soon formed. One group were those were too sick to live, and another group were those who were too weak to live. These two groups were ill and/or wounded or weakened by malnutrition and disease. The other two divisions were more psychological. Many literally gave up when captured, feeling no hope of survival. Finally, there were the prisoners who were determined to live, and they planned and plotted to survive. Their philosophy was that every day was one closer to liberation (Gordon 2011). After they were liberated, many prisoners-of-war credited sheer luck, determination, camaraderie, and friendships as survival techniques. Acceptance of the situation provided the strength to continue as did a conscious will to survive. Being fully aware always, anticipating the guards' next moves, and improvising were survival techniques (MacArthur 2005).

Food was an obsession and a frequent topic of conversation. Sharing recipes was popular, especially recipes that did not include rice. Medical care was very rudimentary. Doctor used razors and knives for surgery, homemade alcohol for anesthesia, and reused bandages. Medical staff soon learned how to create medicine from plants (MacArthur 2005).

Camp clergy sanctioned the use of Bible pages to wrap papaya leaves to create a tobacco substitute with the request that the prisoners read the scriptures on the page before smoking. To ease boredom (and when the prisoners were healthy), baseball games were organized. Occasionally, the guards would play against the POWs, but it was known that the guards had to win. Programs were organized as entertainment as a special treat; the Japanese occasionally showed movies, usually Disney (MacArthur 2005). Improvisation was necessary in the camps. Prisoners built primitive radios that were hidden in pieces from the guards. In several camps, making penicillin from rice mold was accomplished, saving many lives. As clothing wore out (many POWs had never received additional clothing after capture), prisoners figured out how to make sandals from bark and leaves and loincloths from tattered uniforms (MacArthur, 2005). Prisoners quickly learned how to "make do."

WAITING

By the spring of 1945, most prisoners were barely surviving. Many believed that their imprisonment was ending soon in some way. Most POWs were aware of the execution order if the Americans invaded but hung on to the hope that no invasion would be necessary due to the increased American bombings of major Japanese cities.

POW life was a dull routine. The prisoners felt isolated from the world and forgotten. The best morale booster was hearing the American planes flying over Japan after almost three years. As it became obvious that

Japan was losing, the guards' treatment of the prisoners became even harsher in many camps (Gordon 2011).

When the Japanese surrendered, many camp guards feared retaliation from the prisoners. Except for a few isolated cases, the prisoners didn't want revenge. They just wanted to go home. Air drops of barrels filled with clothes, medicine, food, and instructions were soon being delivered to the many camps. Some prisoners became ill by eating too much, but the supplies were welcome. The air drops reassured the POWs that people did indeed care. Liberation was similar to emerging from a long nightmare and was anticlimactic to many POWs. Telegrams were sent home, and life was restarted.

Telling the Story

George Burlage was a career journalist. He worked as a public information officer for forty years, first as a Marine and then for the Federal Aviation Administration. Writing was his life.

Retirement didn't end his writing. George was a frequent contributor to the Denton newspaper and was a frequent guest speaker at veteran and civic events. My daughters and I lived with my dad for twenty years. More days than not, we would return home for the day to the sound of his typing on his old Royal manual typewriter.

George wanted people to know what he experienced as a prisoner-of-war. I don't know if he had a plan or a goal with these writings. It was like he remembered something that happened during those forty months, and he was compelled to describe the event. When typing became difficult for him, he wrote on legal pads. I discovered his POW survival tips written on the back of an envelope that had been stuck into a book on Douglas MacArthur. He filled binders with his memories and kept these in a big storage box in his bedroom closet.

George Burlage passed away in late 2008 after a surgical procedure. It was not expected. In typical George fashion, he had prepared notebooks for me. One had requests for his memorial service. He was to be interred at the Dallas-Fort Worth National Cemetery, and that meant that my mother's ashes (she died thirteen years earlier) had to be moved from our hometown to Dallas. He wanted "Taps" and "The Marines' Hymn" to be played and his Purple Heart group to be honorary pallbearers. Another notebook had financial documents, and the third one contained life advice. The binders were in his closet and labeled. That's when I noticed the big storage box and discovered the stacks of writings and notebooks.

When I decided to start going through the writings, I could hear my dad's voice in my mind. He was always worried that stories like his would be forgotten. I knew what I had to do. I retired after a long teaching career in 2016 and decided that it was time to write this story. Organizing the writings was a major task. I bought folders in several colors and began to group by major topics—childhood, Philippines before the war, Corregidor, early days of capture, various camps, sabotaging (one of his favorite topics), the hell ship experience, Mitsubishi, freedom. My next step was to read the writings and eliminate duplicates. When there were several writings and speeches on the same topic, I combined them by pulling out descriptions, quotes, and events and including them in the narrative. Every quote in this book is directly from writings and are the exact words. There are several quotes that really stuck with me, especially the warnings that George's mentor and sergeant John Hughes gave him about getting off the island of Palawan and his response to the medic who offered him a method to kill himself in the hold of his hell ship. Not every writing went into this book. One example of this is that he became very intrigued by the idea of Japanese corporations paying reparations to their former POW slave laborers. Those were not part of the POW experience narrative, so they were not included in the book.

Many of my dad's accounts touched me deeply. Of course, I knew of his POW experiences. As he aged, we talked frequently about what he had endured. Still, I learned so much about those forty months and as I continued to read through these writings, I developed an even deeper admiration for my father. He was truly a self-made man who enlisted in the Marines to get money to finish college and wound up surviving just about the worst that life can throw at a person. Some of what he wrote really disturbed me, especially his accounts of the hell ship experience. I became angry at the American officials who decided to sacrifice the troops in the Philippines and at MacArthur who deserted those troops. His description of being force-marched through Manila as a prize of war saddened me. Most of all, I marveled at how he mentally and physically recovered from his POW ordeal and lived to be ninety. He fought for survival for almost forty months and as a result, he lived every moment of life in full appreciation.

As I read the accounts, I often gasped at George's descriptive language and imagery. My daughters were barraged by my texts with quotes from their grandpa. His statement about knowing how it would be to be a witness to your own funeral was based on being shoved in the bottom of a hell ship and listening to the hold coverings being winched shut. His admission that to him, every day of freedom is beautiful has become a mantra for me.

This book is not a diary. It is organized chronologically by places and events. I also included telegrams, photos, and letters that my grandmother saved about her Marine son. She never gave up hope even when he was listed as missing-in-action for more than a year. I never met her, but I thank her. Here's an example of how humble my dad was about his war experiences. In the early 2000s, I found his medals, including his Bronze Star and Purple Heart, in a shoe box in a drawer in his room. I also found a plastic bag that had the telegrams, newspaper articles, and photos that his mother had kept during the war. A scrapbook and shadow box display were his Christmas gifts from me that year. Articles written by George are also included in the narrative.

This book is a story of one young man who found himself in a situation that he could have never predicted. When he would speak to my high school history classes, he always began with the statement, "I bet you are wondering how I got myself in this mess." That's what this book is about—how a young Marine survived what many people would consider impossible to survive.

George Burlage never thought of himself as a hero. He always said that he was "just" was serving his country. Many people disagreed, though. At the end of the narrative, I included a tribute to him by former Georgia governor and U.S. Senator Zell Miller and an editorial written in tribute to him by the editor of his former employer, the *Denton Record-Chronicle.*

This is the book that George Burlage should have written but never did. He told me that decades ago when sharing his experiences with a group in his hometown, he was asked why he "let" himself be captured, and that was proof that people didn't really care about this story. No persuasion could change his mind. He said that no one would be interested because this happened so long ago and in a different world. Since he refused, I wrote it for him using his own words. This is the story of a young man who would not have his future stolen from him when he was captured at Corregidor by the Japanese on May 6, 1942. He swore that he would survive. And he did.

Georgianne Burlage
Daughter of George Burlage, Fourth Marines

Prologue

Denton, Texas—my hometown—has an All-War Memorial on the Denton County Courthouse lawn to honor the veterans from our county who served in our nation's wars. It was dedicated in 1996. This verse from Isaiah that summarizes the emotions of war-weary soldiers returning to civilian life is inscribed on the memorial:

"And they shall judge among nations and shall rebuke many people; and I shall beat their swords into plowshares, and their spears into pruning hooks;. nation shall not lift up sword against nation, neither shall they learn war anymore. Isaiah 2:4."

Chapter One

Country Boy

"I had so much to learn. School would be my center of learning ...Any and every subject was new to me."

George Burlage

George Burlage had great plans for his future. He wanted a college education, and he wanted off the family's dairy farm near Visalia, California.

His childhood wasn't a happy one. His father was domineering and cruel, once threatening to cut his son's tongue to stop him from stammering. His older sister was killed when a kerosene lamp exploded in her hands, casting a sorrow over the family that never left. George was the second son and was in his older brother's shadow. He also had two younger sisters.

George graduated from high school in 1937 and from junior college in 1939. He financed his education by working for the National Youth Administration as a school bus driver and school janitor. A college dean paid for one semester's tuition. However,

after his graduation, he needed money to finish college and during the Great Depression, jobs were few.

I was born in 1918 in the farming community of Ivanhoe near Visalia, California, in the San Joaquin Valley and a child of the Great Depression. I was named after my father, George, but my middle name, Edward, was in honor of an uncle. Rebecca Crawford Burlage, my mother, was a several-generations Visalia native, and my father was the son of a German immigrant who settled in Missouri. My mother was several years younger than my dad. I was the third oldest child and the second son, a difficult place in the family hierarchy.

When I started grammar school, I didn't even know who I was. In fact, I had a fight over who I thought I was and who I wasn't. The teacher had placed the names of the first graders on the blackboard and then told us to pick out our names. That's when the confusion began.

I decided that I was Stanfield Smith. The name looked so pretty spelled out among the others. Scholarly Stanfield claimed it just as I did. I don't know what I was thinking because I had never been taught how to think. After a little scuffle with Stanfield, he remained Stanfield, and dumb old me became George. The other six first graders—there were eight of us—knew who they were.

I had so much to learn. School would be my center of learning for the next eight years. Any and every subject was new for me. I had never been taught anything at home. I did not know my numbers or my ABCs. Often, as in my farm family, there wasn't time for parents to read "Mother Goose" stories or "The Three Little Bears" to the kids. The idea was "when you get to school, you'll be taught those things."

My school was East Lynne and was administered by Tulare County. Schools were located approximately five- to six-miles apart so that the pupils would have no more than two and a half to three miles to walk. Most schools were the same: two rooms with each having four grades. East Lynne had a roll portion which could be raised to combine the two rooms. There was no running water; the two rear corner areas of the school grounds each boasted a six- hole privy, one for the boys and one for the girls. A handpump in the school's front yard provided the only water for drinking and washing hands if needed.

Mrs. Scott was my first-grade teacher and my second, third, and fourth. She was ageless, and I thought she looked like George Washington. Mrs. Swain was my fifth, sixth, and seventh grade teacher, and then Mrs. Duran returned to the school for my eighth-grade year.

At the time I started school, the family lived on the Barlow Ranch. I was born in the ranch house. We grew mostly fruit on the 120-acre farm. It was part of the Visalia Independent School District. Our family consisted of my father George Stefan, mother Cora Rebecca (Becky) Crawford Burlage, brother Bob who was known as "Sonny," my sisters Ruth and Lois, and me. My father was the son of a German immigrant and was born in Missouri. When he was a young man, the riches of the West summoned him. He claimed to have ridden a bicycle that he named "Blue Flyer" to California, but I doubt it for many reasons, mainly having to cross the Rocky Mountains. I remember when Lois was born in a midwife's home in Visalia. My father drove Sonny, Ruth, and me into town in our buggy to see my mother and new sister.

My older sister Louise Esther had died tragically in 1924 a few months before Lois's arrival. From an early age, Louise had to do a large amount of the housework. As she lit a kerosene lamp one evening, she somehow ignited her dress and as the fire blazed up her clothes, she ran outside with clothing ablaze. The blaze was probably intensified by the kerosene that was on her clothing. I had just stepped into the kitchen through the back door when she ran past with Harve Scott, who stayed with us and worked full-time on the ranch, trying to catch her. Louise fell, and Harve picked her up and put her in a nearby horse trough full of water. She was taken in the house and doctored with oil. (I remember that it was kept in a gallon glass bottle and was used in some of the machinery.) She was finally taken the hospital in Visalia where she died the next day. I can still see her badly burned body lying on the bed being treated with that oil.

This tragedy truly changed the family. It was also a tragedy because it didn't have to happen. Too much was demanded of Louise for a child of twelve. Most of all was the fact that electric lines ran within a few feet of the house, but my father had taken no initiative to bring electrical use into our house. The gloom which overcame the house remained forever and had an everlasting effect on all of us.

My father was the foreman of the Barlow Ranch operations. We had migrant workers come from Mexico in the fall to help with picking the fruit. During harvest season, there were at least a dozen workers involved. Mother fed them at noontime. Workers would come to the house when the noon whistle sound was heard (the whistle was from a steam laundry in Visalia which was heard for miles), filled a washbasin with water from a hand pump, and dried off with an endless roll of cloth towels. Mother financed the grocery bill with eggs. She had quite a few laying hens, and she swapped eggs for groceries. The only thing modern in the house was a telephone. She would ring the store in Visalia to order groceries. Soon, a man in his Model T delivery truck would drive into the yard, unload the groceries, and pick up the eggs.

In the first few days of first grade, I walked home after school with a neighbor kid. Every day when we came to the intersection of Lovers and Sauerkraut Lanes, he would knock me down and jump on me. A neighbor farmer had a vineyard at this juncture and observed one incident and hurried over to our house to tell my dad about the daily occurrence. Then after I got home, Dad was waiting with a warning of "The next time that bastard does that to you and you don't fight back, I'll give you a beating you'll remember. I will do it every day until you fight back." I never got that beating because the next day, I jumped on him, knocked him down, and urinated on him. The tattletale neighbor saw it all and couldn't wait to tell my dad. I never said a word.

In late 1924, we moved to another farm, but I didn't have to change schools. We had a share-lease arrangement on the new farm. Initially, we grew peaches and prunes, but we soon added a dairy and double-cropped the orchards with alfalfa. I was six years old at the time. My father got a 2 x 4, cut off two pieces, made a T-milk stool, gave me a bucket, set me under a cow, and said "Pull." I pulled for nine years at 5:15 every morning and 5:00 pm every evening.

I walked about two and a half miles to school each way. I loved walking home. It was a pleasure having that experience of almost bumping my nose against those beautiful Sierra Nevada mountains.

Being tongue-tied was a real obstacle in the classroom. Mrs. Scott would pass over me in our class recitation, but she sometimes tried to understand me. Finally, in desperation she drove out to see my parents to find out why they were not trying to help me. The trip was futile. Dad didn't believe in doctors, dentists, or preachers and sought no solution to my problem. I could have been the village idiot for all he showed. He threatened more than once to split my tongue to "cure" my tongue-tied speech.

After I finished eighth grade at East Lynne, I began Visalia High School. High school was uneventful. There was a real divide between those of us from the county schools and those from the city schools. I didn't participate in sports because I spent the early mornings and late afternoons under a cow, pulling. My only organized activity in high school was with 4H Club. There were meetings and picnics to attend and enjoy. I raised a hog each year for the fat hog competition and one year showed the grand championship barrow. As a future farmer, I also took a pen of three hogs to the Interstate Livestock Show (made of competitors from California, Oregon, and Idaho) in San Francisco and won prizes. I quit this when I started junior college.

Three of the five of us who went to high school from East Lynne graduated from high school. I was the only one to continue my education. In the fall of 1939, I enrolled at Visalia Junior College (now the College of the Sequoias). I began to ease out of the milking responsibilities when I got into a real study pattern in junior college.

The effects of the Great Depression cannot be exaggerated. I remember the influx of Steinbeck "Okies" and their looking for work in the new "promised land" of California. Our family always had plenty to eat because we were on a farm and my mom always had a pot of red beans on the stove for hungry people. During my junior college days, and especially in the summers, I tried to get work to save money to finish at a four-year college. There were rare jobs, ranging from fifteen to twenty-five cents an hour. I worked at Rocky Hill Farms one summer, a dairy that produced certified milk. One of the requirements of producing certified milk was that the cows had to be milked by hand instead of by machine. I certainly had experience milking. Work hours were from sunrise to sundown, board and room, for a $1.50 a day. At the end of the fourth day, I collected my six dollars and went home. That wasn't a job – it was an example of a business taking advantage of hungry, Depression-ridden jobseekers.

Because I was totally broke, I was set to leave junior college at the end of the freshman year. I had a counseling session with my English teacher (also the Dean of Women) at which I told her I was leaving. When I told her the reason – that I was broke—she reached into her desk for her checkbook and wrote me a check for twenty dollars and promised that I would have a job with the NYA (National Youth Administration), a New Deal program to financially help college students. I did various jobs from helping at night school to lawn care at twenty-five cents an hour. I walked home on the nights I worked in the gym— nine miles.

I applied for and got one of the bus driver jobs at the high school. This paid thirty dollars a month for two hours' work a day. One experience stands out during my year of driving. One morning after a heavy early rain, I hit high water on a rural road, and the bus stalled. A farmer saw my troubles and rescued the students by pulling his horse-drawn wagon alongside and took them to higher ground to board another bus dispatched for them. They were a bit late for class, but they had a good story to tell. I also was a member of the cross-country team in junior college. Truthfully, I was an adequate runner, but I enjoyed competing.

Graduation was a happy/sad occasion—glad that I was halfway to a bachelor's degree but sad because two-year friendships and camaraderie were ending. I had plans to continue my education at Fresno State but couldn't raise enough cash to attend.

Chapter Two

Travel, Adventure, Romance

"The recruiter promised me that I would be a pilot in months. I didn't even get on a plane until after I was liberated and flew home."

George Burlage

The U.S. Marine Corps and the recruiter's promise of flight training gave George hope. The Marines were an elite group and although Germany had annexed parts of Europe and Japan had invaded China, Americans believed that the United States could avoid hostilities. The recruiter guaranteed travel, romance, and adventure in the Marine Corps, and George certainly wanted all three.

He graduated from Boot Camp in San Diego in early September 1939. War had broken out in Europe, but George was on his way to Asia—far from Europe and Hitler. A tropical paradise in the American-owned Philippines awaited him.

In the summer of 1939, I went to Los Angeles to look for a job to save up to finish college. Early in August, I was wandering down on a downtown street when I spotted a recruitment poster and stopped to admire the painting that was displayed. Two Marines in fresh starched khakis were raising the American flag over a beautiful tropical island. The poster's banner headline proclaimed, "Travel, Adventure, Romance: The United States Marine Corps."

A voice behind me said, "Lad, would you like to be one of us?" It was a Marine recruiter. I told him that I had an associate degree and was waiting to hear from the Army Air Corps about flight training at Randolph Field in San Antonio. With disdain, the recruiter looked at me and said, "Why fool with the Army? With your education, you will be flying in six months with us." These recruiters were looking for strong farm boys who came to the city to start a new life. I enlisted for four years at a pay of $21 a month plus room, board, and travel and was one of six applicants who passed training out of a hundred who applied to the USMC on that date.

Boot camp was accelerated due to war beginning in Europe on September 1, 1939, and the training and survival skills learned helped me during my captivity. The USMC discipline toughed me, too. Soon after boot camp graduation, our training platoon, Number 27, left San Diego aboard the *USS Lexington* (it was sunk in 1942 at the Battle of the Coral Sea) for Bremerton, Washington. Duty on the ship was short. In a few weeks, many of us in the platoon were transferred to Mare Island in San Francisco Bay for additional transfer to an Asiatic Station. The Marines went aboard the *USS Henderson*, one of the Navy's two transports. It had been used in World War I. I sailed out of San Francisco for a two-year Asia tour of duty. It would turn out to be six years before I would return to the United States. My first stop was Honolulu after nine days at sea. The ship tied up at Aloha Tower, which was a major landmark. I spent the last of my money on a sightseeing trip around Oahu.

From Hawaii, it was a two-week trip to Guam where there was an exchange of Marines stationed at the small guard garrison located there. Personnel assignments were determined for the Fourth Marines to be sent to Cavite, Philippines (the Philippines were an American territory at that time) or to Shanghai, China, for the embassy duty at Peking (Beijing) or Tientsin. I departed the ship at the Manila piers on January 3, 1940, right across the bay from Cavite for what was to be a two-year duty in the Philippines, a tour whose ending I never foresaw. I was going to a tropical paradise.

Chapter Three

The Good Life

"Life as an American Marine had been the promised land of travel, adventure, and romance. Cavite was a remote idyllic location."
George Burlage

George Burlage arrived at the Cavite Navy Yard in the American-controlled Philippines in the late fall of 1939. He was to be in the Philippines for two years, and he would return to the U.S to complete his enlistment in December 1941.

Cavite and the Philippines were similar to a recruiting poster —palm trees, tropical sun, white-washed Spanish style buildings. George enjoyed these years in the Philippines which was an American Commonwealth at the time. He was on the Cavite Town Patrol, and the area was so tranquil that he made his rounds on a bicycle. The biggest issues were Marines and sailors getting into drunken fights at the local bars. Horse and buggy taxis waited by the front gate of the navy yard to take the Marines to the local clubs and dance halls. The Philippines were an entirely new world compared to the San Joaquin Valley in California.

Life in the Philippines was slow paced and enjoyable until December 8, 1941, when the idyllic days came to a crashing end.

When I arrived at Cavite on January 3, 1940, it was going back to what I had pictured as turn-of-the-century military post. There were 23,000 Americans based in the Philippines—18,500 Army personnel and 3,500 Navy sailors and Marines. I entered an era of where the 170 Marines stationed here depicted what was pictured on the 1930s recruiting posters – my wearing wash khaki uniforms topped with the traditional "campaign hat" (what is the drill instructor's hat now). Even in the tropical heat, the field scarf (tie) complete with battle insignia was worn for both duty and liberty. This was the time before dungarees, and khaki was always worn. Each Marine had one pair of bib overalls for extremely dirty work— which was seldom. Boom docker shoes/boots were not yet a quartermaster issue; the high-top dress shoe was the only one available. All socks were white in color. A Marine usually had two pairs of shoes —a new pair for wearing on duty, liberty, and for inspections and the older pair for wearing on training exercises and work details. An old pair was often referred to as "campaign shoes."

Our weapons were left from other wars— the Boxer Rebellion in China, Spanish-American War, Philippines Insurrection, and World War I. The 1903 Springfield rifle (with a 24-inch bayonet) was issued in boot camp and was your best friend as long as you remained in the Corps. Additionally, in Cavite we had water-cooled .40- caliber machine guns, a few BARs, Lewis machine guns, and Thompson submachine guns. Another weapon was the three-inch siege gun, once used to breach walls in the Boxer Rebellion. In almost ritualistic fashion, the siege guns were taken out of quartermaster storage at least once each year, and a few rounds were fired by Marine gun crews. I am sure that the ammunition was as old as the guns.

As a footnote to the siege guns, I have this observation. When I was departing Bataan in January 1942 to join the beach defense at Corregidor, I saw the remnants of these guns. Heading for the barge, which was tied up in the Mariveles Harbor, I passed the partially destroyed guns and dozens of spent shell casings. It appeared that a Japanese bomb and artillery fire had destroyed both guns and ammunition. It was remarkable how they got to Bataan and for what use they were intended.

Also, the two-man crew of the water-cooled .30-caliber moved their equipment on two carts. One was for the machine gun, and the other carried the water cans and ammunition. These were quite impressive in a parade as the machine gunners pulled their carts in formation.

And how was transportation accomplished in those days? First, if there was a boat of any kind, it was used. If the distance was too far, marching became the next choice. Last, and only when necessary, motor transport was used. Airplanes were for fighting, not for transporting people. In Cavite the motor pool consisted of two trucks, one very old and one a bit newer. One of these was necessary to transport the guard to Sangley Point each day. The fourteen Marines making up the town patrol (including me) had one bicycle for running errands. In the evenings, there was a driver and his *calesa* (horse-drawn, two-wheel cart) standing by to take a patrolman to the scene of disturbance.

The formal designation of the station was the Marine Barracks, U.S. Navy Yard, Cavite, and the principal duty was guarding the Navy Yard and the installations at Sangley Point (where fuel storage, Naval Hospital, radio communications towers, and the PBY— flying boat airplanes Squadron were located). Marines also ran the Navy Prison (one of the three the Navy had at the time) located in the Spanish-built Fort San Felipe, and the Marine Patrol (military police unit) operated out of Porta Vega, which was completed by the Spanish in 1602 to guard the entrance to Cavite Island.

The city of Cavite, across the bay from Manila, consisted of three barrios: Cavite, San Roque, and Caridad. Cavite was a small island reached from San Roque by a short causeway. Foot traffic entered the island through the salliport in the center of the fortification and vehicular traffic was around the ends of the fort. The Navy Yard occupied about half of the lower (south) end of thc island. The barrio was old, dating back to the early Spanish days. A seawall of large quarried stone encircled the island. Bacoor Bay (part of the larger Manila Bay) was on the east and Canacao Bay, which lies between Cavite and Sangley Point, is west. Canacao Bay is where the Spanish Fleet took refuge in the battle with Dewey's forces during the Spanish-American War. Pan American Airlines also used Sangley Point for its clipper ships when it initiated air travel to Asia in the 1930s.

While the principal duty was to guard, Marines were conspicuous elsewhere. In addition to the Brig and the Town Patrol, Marines were assigned orderly duties to the Commandment, 16th Naval District, and on the Navy ferry that operated several trips a day between Cavite and Manila. The ferry was the principal liberty transportation to Manila, and sometimes an MP had to keep order. When the Navy established an underground communication station on Corregidor in the late 1930s, Marines were assigned guard duty there. Marines rotated between Cavite and "the Rock" (Corregidor) every few weeks. When Germany occupied most of Europe in the early stages of World War II, ships of several occupied countries were in Manila Bay. A Marine guard was assigned to each of the ships (which stayed at anchor) to keep the crews on the "right side."

Cavite duty was good. House boys kept barracks clean, shoes shined, and laundry done. All the Marines had to do was to be present for duty. With all this help, we always tried to look sharp—and we did. Payday was twice a month in pesos. Several people sat at the pay table. The pay clerk handed the private his seventeen to eighteen pesos (insurance had been deducted), and the others started taking it two pesos for houseboy, two for laundry, three for Navy Relief, one for the Mestizo Fund, etc. A Marine was living high if he qualified for the rifle range. It meant an extra six pesos for a sharpshooter and ten for the expert. Sometimes, Marines got nicked for something acquired from the quartermaster (paying cash or taken out of the clothing allowance). Once I paid thirty cents to the quartermaster for a first-aid kit packet which I used in an emergency to stop bleeding from a bad cut. The kit, which everyone carried on his web belt, was surplus from World War I. The quartermaster said that I shouldn't have used it if I didn't want to pay for it.

Liberty wasn't a big deal with most Marines. A little Genebra gin, rum, or beer drinking was a payday routine for many. Dreamland Cabaret was a big attraction both for sailors and for Marines where dozens of girls danced for ten centavos a dance. It was a place where sailors and Marines didn't always mix (quite common in those days), but the presence of the town patrol usually kept or restored things to order. Dreamland was owned by an American who was respected for the dignity he displayed at the Cabaret. The band always could sense the mood of the crowd and the proper tempo to the music. In those days the Navy and Marines had a preponderance of Texans, and "San Antonio Rose" was heard quite often. There was always that happy, go-getting drunk Texan who kept things going by shouting when the music began, "Stand up, you son-of-a-bitch. That's the national anthem."

Then there were the inspected prostitutes. At this time, there were five recognized houses of prostitution (Navy inspected) with Filipino girls who had to meet certain requirements set down by the Navy medical people. To enforce the rules, the Town Patrol was charged with checking the cleanliness of the houses and assuring that girls were certified each week by Navy Medical. For nearly a year, it was my job to check the houses (I traveled on a bicycle) and make sure that the thirty to forty girls went to the Navy Dispensary each week for their exams and shots.

The big "togetherness" event each week was the parade field review. We did at times get a spurt in training. Gunner Olin L Beall (who retired with about forty years after Korea duty as a colonel) was the self-proclaimed master with the bayonet. He had the idea all Marines should also be masters at bayoneting. More time was spent running around the parade field with rifles at high point for some misplaced thrust than was spent in actual training.

Gunner Beall did not appeal to everyone because he was always bragging about himself and his duties in just about all of the "banana wars" (the wars in Central America during American imperialism), but I will personally vouch for him as a real Marine with a true concern for his men. He took six of us PRCs with him one weekend to the Naval Reservation at Mariveles. At this time there was nothing there but a few Filipino poachers and squatters. We traveled in what was called a "680 boat"—a utility- type craft for moving a few people but mostly for towing barges. The next day when we started back, the 680, due to high winds, had been anchored about 200 yards offshore. The skipper, a Filipino in the U.S. Navy, evidently was asleep. We needed to get aboard and head back to Cavite because a typhoon was slipping up on us. Yelling did no good, and pistol shots failed to awaken the skipper. Finally, the gunner stripped off his clothing and swam the choppy waters to the boat. The skipper was trying to protect the boat from being damaged at the docks, so the gunner didn't criticize him. The trip back to Cavite was in total darkness with high winds and waves. If we hadn't gotten underway when we did, we could have been in grave danger.

Except for a few overnight bivouacs that included marching to a site, there was little other training. One attempt at a beach landing had a sergeant in charge. He loaded us in a forty-foot whale boat, the last one of the water-cooled .30-calibers placed in the bow and told the Navy coxswain to head for an area where we would land at Sangley Point. En route he instructed us to keep our rifles dry by holding them with one hand at arm's length over our heads as we used the other hand to pivot over the gunwales into the water. Then we were to wade ashore. Except for our sergeant, all the Marines were watching the coxswain pivot over the side, but he was the only one to leave the boat. The only thing visible in the water was his campaign hat floating by and him swimming ashore. The coxswain brought the boat in, and we disembarked in the waist-deep shallow water. It was a short exercise.

As time went on, things began to change. The less than two hundred Marine barracks personnel were growing in numbers, eventually bringing the count to battalion strength. The designation was changed to 1st Separate Marine Battalion (Provisional Anti-Aircraft). Gun emplacements were constructed along the beaches, and 3-inch, .50- caliber antiaircraft guns were installed. Of course, as with the rest of our ammunition, these guns had been obsolete for years, having been removed from World War I ships. We even received a rangefinder to go with them and some old ammunition which gave us an altitude range very short of what was required for antiaircraft defense. We believed that we were ready for a possible attack. We never expected what would really happen.

One fellow Marine who I met at Cavite became an important friend after we were captured. He was Platoon Sergeant John Hughes. We became friends when we served in the Town Patrol, and as he thought that I had potential in the Corps, he often gave me advice. Hughes was from the mountains of West Virginia and had participated in campaigns in Nicaragua and China during his enlistment in the 1920s. He was one of the Marines' top pistol shots, and he understood people and had served several enlistments. Although he had only a basic education, he had an uncanny wisdom with much psychology thrown in. I admired his leadership and his example. He was my mentor.

I have three more observations about Cavite:

1. Olongapo. This was sort of an exile for Marines whom the officers didn't want at Cavite. The rifle range was just down the road, and there was a bar run by a Chinese man who worked a long pay-out chit system for thirsty Cavite Marines. I went on several details to the area, particularly Grande Island, where there was some thought of placing .50 -caliber antiaircraft defense. The Philippine army had a battery of 1878-model disappearing guns here.
2. Genebra Gin. This was the favorite hard drink distilled in the Philippines and the cause of trouble for most who got in trouble. There was a belief that the alcohol used in trucks, buses, and the few cars and Genebra Gin came out of the same spigot at the

distillery. If it were in a bottle with a label on it, it was Genebra but if in a barrel, it was "locomotive gin" to the average person. Most servicemen thought there was no difference in quality.

3. We were "reassured" about a possible attack by the Japanese with statements like "they have small eyes and can't see or fly at night" and "we'll defeat them in six weeks." It turned out that the Japanese could see extremely well and were very good pilots.

Life as an American Marine in pre-World War II Philippines had been the promised land of travel, adventure, and romance. Cavite was an idyllic remote location. The Marines were there to protect our possession, the American Philippine Islands. I had truly enjoyed my two years in the Philippines before the war came to the islands. It was a pleasant tour-of-duty, but I was ready to come back to the United States to finish my four-year enlistment. I had moved out of the barracks and was waiting transport home on December 8, 1941, when my tropical paradise was attacked by the Imperial Japanese forces.

A LETTER HOME BEFORE THE OUTBREAK OF WAR

Not too long before the attack on Cavite, George Burlage sent this letter to his Uncle Milton Crawford in Visalia, California. This was his last communication with his family for almost two years. The letter was published in the *Visalia Times-Delta* in late December 1941.

FORMER STUDENT, WITH MARINES IN WAR ZONE, WRITES FOLKS

OF LIFE JUST BEFORE JAP ATTACK ON MANILA

(The following letter, written November 18 at Cavite, near Manila, by George Burlage, son of Mr. and Mrs. George S. Burlage of Ivanhoe, was received by J. Milton (Sam) Crawford, his uncle, this Monday. The letter was in route nearly a month and a half. It gives a colorful picture of life in and around Manila just before the Japanese let go. Burlage, who graduated from high school and junior college here, enlisted in Uncle Sam's Marines three years ago. Here's his letter:)

To keep up with the only social obligation that I have left, I will endeavor to write you. Also, about this time of year, we start to think of Christmas and all the folks at home which also gets one in the writing mood. It seems that although this is the scene of excitement at times, one never forgets home, even though we do let our correspondence lag.

Talk about excitement, there was plenty of it around here last week as the great event in the life of the Filipinos for the year took place. I am referring to the annual fiesta which brings thousands of people into Cavite for the fiesta events every year. This is an ancient religious affair which brings in most of the natives within traveling distance of the city. They all come to worship and pray for the Patron Saint, the Virgin of Solitude, in the ancient church of Porta Vega. The city of 30,000 persons swelled with enormous crowds blocking all vehicular travel.

This picturesque fiesta is followed with the religious fervor almost incomparable. Every year it seems to bring contentment for the poor. They come and give their meager savings to the church and go back home for another year of mere existence. I guess that they should be happy as this is the only time of the year that these people get away from their native barrios and travel a few kilometers in caravans, buses, or even carabao carts.

Together with the crowds come the inevitable beggars and vendors that are so common in the Orient. Beggars of whom a person who has been to the Orient can't describe lined both sides of the street from the Fort to Porta Vega across the Isthmus del Rosario, which connects the island of Cavite to the mainland. Vendors crowded into every corner and even pushed one another's wares out into the street to make room for someone else's stands. An assortment of bright colored improvised shades were put up to ward off the tropical sun. Just picture a public market in Arabia, and you have the setting of the scene. Surely these people copied the habits of the Moros of another region of the Southern islands of the Philippines.

Together with all this, the natives have a great feast making up for all they lack during the past year. Everyone I know is invited. I accepted an invitation to eat at the home of Filipinos, whom I have known since I've been here. They had all of their relatives from the province totaling around thirty people. I sat down to a table of roast pig (cooked on a stick over an open fire), fried chicken, and native fruits. Anything that I wanted I could get because I was the guest; an American in their home at fiesta time, the honor was all theirs.

Recently on November 10, we celebrated the Marine Corps birthday, another great event for us in Cavite. Special dinner, sports events, and a general good time was had by all. Throughout the events our motto, Semper Fidelis, seems to stand out more and more. It takes a little celebration like that to make a person proud of the organization he serves.

Blackout exercises are still very popular out here. We have them ranking from fifteen minutes up to two hours duration. This coming Friday, the first nationwide all blackout exercises will be held. We will be on duty as always, and I'm curious just to see how this is going to turn out. All the rest of the blackouts have been very successful.

The importing of food into the Philippines is really off. Even the service has had to go without a balanced diet occasionally. Rice is very common, of course, to see on the table now. It also makes me think of home and good things to eat. So with the thought of home and good chow, I will close this lengthy letter.

Sincerely,

George Burlage

A cable dated out of Manila on December 22 from the writer of this letter to relatives here has been received, indicating that George was still all right as of that date.

Chapter Four

Paradise Lost

> "I wanted you to see what real courage is, instead of getting the idea that courage is a man with a gun in his hand. It's when you know you're licked before you begin but you begin anyway, and you see it through no matter what. You rarely win, but sometimes you do."
> Atticus Finch, *To Kill a Mockingbird* by Harper Lee

Most of the Marines and sailors at Cavite had no difficulty in comprehending why sirens were sounding on December 10, 1941. There had been sightings of Japanese planes the previous two days, and the men at Cavite knew that there would be an attack soon. Indeed, Cavite was the bullseye for scores of Japanese bombers on December 10, and the base was destroyed.

The American planes on the ground at nearby Clark Field had nine hours after Pearl Harbor was bombed to be flown to a safe location. General MacArthur's hesitancy in ordering an evacuation resulted in the loss of most of the air fleet in the Philippines. Other American bases on Luzon were attacked the same day, resulting in the loss of the American planes.

The Philippines was only one of the many targets for the Japanese. Pearl Harbor, Hong Kong, the American bases in the Philippines and on Guam and Wake islands, Singapore—Asian possessions of the Dutch, British, and Americans—were attacked, and the results were the same. Japan was claiming "Asia for Asians," and they were succeeding.

The unprepared Marines and sailors stationed on the Filipino bases were armed with World War I-era weapons. The antiaircraft batteries' range was too low to reach the Japanese bombers. The outcome was never in doubt.

On December 10, 1941, I quickly realized that there was another side to this idyllic life.

After I arrived in the Philippines in early 1940, I soon became aware of how woefully unprepared the United States was for war. I really didn't believe that the US thought that Japan would involve us in their aggression although the brutal invasion of Nanjing should have concerned us. War was coming. It was obvious.

How unprepared were we? Our weapons were from World War I. The entire Marine Corps had fewer members than the New York City police. We didn't even have a jeep at Cavite, and I shared a bicycle for Town Patrol. We were told that the Japanese would be no match for us. It turned out to be the opposite. The situation began to intensify when the remaining Fourth Marines were sent to the Philippines from Shanghai, and dependent wives and children were sent back to the States. I, too, was going to be sent home in late December 1941 and didn't plan to stay in the Philippines for much longer.

As the threat of war increased in the Pacific, we Marines at Cavite had been reorganized into a provisional antiaircraft battalion, using 3-inch .50-caliber guns that had been used by the Navy in World War I. Every weapon was outdated: the .03 (1903) Springfield rifles, .30- caliber water-cooled machine guns, and siege guns left over from the Boxer

Rebellion. Needless to say, we weren't prepared for what was being unleashed on us.

My two years in the Philippines had truly been the promised travel, adventure, romance, but I quickly realized that there was an entirely different view when fifty-four Japanese bombers attacked Cavite. Cavite had made a few war preparations like building air raid shelters. The Japanese had already attacked most of our airfields on Luzon by the time Cavite was bombed. When the attack began on December 10, 1942, we were suddenly awakened and issued gas masks. Our old bugler was blowing like mad, trying to wake us up. My first reaction was that the man was drunk and having some fun. After the gas masks were distributed, a truck backed into camp with its lights out, and helmets and live ammunition were given to us. That's when we knew it was for real. Pearl Harbor had been attacked, and the fear was that we would be next. There were twenty-three officers and 708 enlisted man in the Marine Battalion at Cavite. At the top of the Bataan Peninsula in the Subic Bay area, forty-eight officers and 718 men from the Fourth Marines had just arrived from Shanghai.

Fifty-four bombers attacked Cavite on December 10. The Japanese forces had also attacked Pearl Harbor (December 7 in Hawaii due to the International Date Line), Hong Kong, Singapore, and Malaya, flying several runs. Our anti-aircraft guns had a maximum reach of 9,000 feet, and the Japanese flew much higher than that. We didn't hit a plane. Scratch one US Navy Yard. Also, scratch our food supply. We were cut to half-rations. Our base was out of operations. A few days later, the bombers returned to hit the fuel depot and radio station. Cavite had been destroyed. A toy pistol would have damaged the Japanese planes as much as we did with our antiquated defenses. It was difficult to hear the planes or the sirens over the roar of the flames that were consuming the navy yard.

After the first bombing, a few other Marines and I found an abandoned truck and decided to drive to a nearby town to search for food. We didn't find much. We returned to the ruins of Cavite with cases of liquor, canned salmon, and pork and beans. The Filipino stores never kept much in stock, but we got what we could. That small amount of food was going to need to last for several weeks because our food supply warehouse had been destroyed.

I tried to keep busy. All I could think of that day was that the war had finally begun, and we weren't ready. hadn't enlisted to be in a war, honestly. President Roosevelt had promised that we would stay out of this war, but Pearl Harbor changed that. I had enlisted for employment and college money.

I wasn't optimistic. I had been taught that Marines never surrendered, but I was realistic. I knew that the Americans and Filipinos were outnumbered and scarce on food and supplies. I also knew how long it took for reinforcements, supplies, and additional troops to reach the Philippines. The future didn't look promising. I faced the fact that the American Navy— if there was one after Pearl Harbor—could not send a convoy to help us. We also knew that the Japanese controlled the Western Pacific and most of the Asian mainland. It wasn't a comforting realization.

Things looked bad for us. Later, I learned that Bataan and Corregidor were called "The Alamo of the Pacific," which is an accurate description. We were supposed to be holding off the Japanese forces to give American forces time to regroup, much like Colonel Travis's situation at the Alamo against the Mexican Army. We were greatly outnumbered and had no hope of additional supplies or reinforcements. Also, we learned later that the Allies had decided to concentrate on Europe and Hitler first to assist the British. We were alone and targeted.

We were marooned. The Japanese had bombed the American bases in the Philippines, resulting in total destruction. Our planes had been caught by bombers at Clark Field and the other bases and never even had a chance to get into the air.

Yet, Marines supposedly never surrendered. I didn't feel very hopeful for my future. I was in a situation that didn't appear to have a good conclusion. However, no one could have predicted what the future actually had planned for us.

Chapter Five

Corregidor Bound

> "My experiences were hard to discuss and even harder to explain. I had witnessed torture, execution, and brutality and watched my friends die one by one. . .This was difficult for people to understand."
>
> George Burlage

War had arrived suddenly in the Philippines, and neither the military nor the civilians were prepared. General Douglas MacArthur, who was living in a luxurious penthouse at the Manila Hotel with his wife and young son, declared Manila an open city hoping to minimize damage to it. He then moved his family (along with his son's amah) to Malinta Tunnel on Corregidor.

The Americans' strategy to combat the Japanese invaders was establishing defensive positions on the Bataan Peninsula and to hold those positions until reinforcements arrived.

George Burlage and the remaining displaced Marines were sent to Bataan to assist with setting up beach defenses. However, General MacArthur believed that the Marines were of little assis-

tance and after three weeks were sent to Corregidor to prepare for a future Japanese invasion.

My unit was moved to Bataan when it was obvious that Manila was going to fall under Japanese control. General MacArthur had declared Manila to be an open city in the attempt to prevent the destruction of the Philippines capital. The Japanese ignored the declaration and bombed Manila. When it became evident that Manila would fall under Japanese control, MacArthur pulled the troops into prearranged positions across the Bataan Peninsula from the China Sea to the top of Manila Bay. Mariveles, at the tip of the peninsula, became an operating base for what was left of the U.S. Navy in Asia—the riverboats from China duty, minesweepers, and one-gun tenders. The Marines from the destroyed Cavite Navy Yard were ordered in late December to help with setting up the defensive line on Bataan. I made the day long trip riding on the top of a supply truck.

The Bataan Peninsula years earlier had been designated as the defensive line against any invading troops. The hope was to hold that line until reinforcements could arrive. The original plan was to establish the line across the northern part of the peninsula, but we didn't have enough weapons for an area that large. We set up more south in the Mount Samat area. Our World War I era water-cooled machine guns were inadequate in any sort of mobile defense because these guns had been designed for trench warfare. The Marines were just in the way.

We were originally supposed to remain on Bataan until reinforcements arrived, but MacArthur didn't want the Marines there. We were wearing khaki uniforms and dress shoes and had no combat gear at all. After three weeks at Bataan, we were sent to Corregidor to set up beach defenses. The Springfield weapons were transported on carts to Mariveles and were placed on barges to be transported the three miles across Manila Bay to Corregidor. Upon arrival, we were assigned to Battery Point.

All of us were part of the Fourth Marines, and several other Fourth Marines had arrived from Shanghai to join us. The well-organized and better prepared Philippine Scouts led by American officers and the 31st Infantry formed the main defense line at Corregidor. These guys had more enthusiasm than training. The Fourth Marines in the Mariveles area were soon joined by an additional three officers, 72 enlisted men, and the Marines from Cavite (I was in this group). The Cavite forces were absorbed into the Fourth Marines as the regiment's Third Battalion. The Fourth Marines were then brought into MacArthur's United States Army Forces in the Far East (USAFFE). Our principal mission was to set up beach defenses on Corregidor because we knew that the Japanese would eventually land there. Corregidor was well-fortified against traditional artillery, but we knew that we were fighting a different type of war.

A little background about Corregidor. Corregidor and Carabao Island were part of the American acquisition of the Philippine Islands after the Spanish-American War. These islands were fortified so that the Americans could protect Manila Bay. Fort Frank and Fort Hughes were constructed on Carabao Island, a 45- acre island with high cliffs located in the Bay. When the Japanese attacked in 1941-1942, the ammunition and heavy guns were practically useless. The weapons were designed as armor-piercing because at the time of the forts' construction in the early 1900s, battleships were a threat. Few preparations had been made for air attacks and high artillery.

Then there was strange, odd Fort Drum. Fort Drum was literally a concrete battleship. A small island had been leveled and then built back up to resemble a battleship. It was a sea fort with twin turrets, 14-inch guns, and a top deck forty or so feet above the water. Military personnel were stationed inside the concrete hull to man the weapons. As with the other Manila Bay installations, it was designed for sea battles, not for antiaircraft artillery.

Corregidor had also been designed to protect Manila Bay. Again, as with the other islands, its defenses were designed for a different type of war, not one with air attacks. The tadpole-shaped "head" faces the South China Sea and is very mountainous. There are only three areas where a landing could happen, and I was placed at one of those, Battery Point. The main sections of the island were tagged Topside, Middleside, and Bottomside. The North and South docks and Malinta Tunnel were the main areas of the island.

Corregidor was nicknamed "The Gibraltar of the East" and was equipped with forty-five coastal guns and mortars organized into 23 groups along with72 anti-aircraft guns in thirteen additional batteries. Two 12-inch battery guns had a range of 29,000 yards. In addition to this, there were the three smaller islands (Forts Drum, Mills, and Frank) that were also heavily fortified. There were major problems with the gun power, though. Most of the guns were fixed and could not be moved. Also, there would be no additional supplies, and the weapons were decades old and ineffective.

The island served as an armed protection for Manila and Manila Bay, and coastal artillery had been fortified and fixed when the Philippines became an American territory. I had been to Corregidor in 1940 to assist in the installation of an underground radio on the island.

My group was instructed to place our outdated antiaircraft weapons on the beaches as a defense and to use the ammunition sparingly. I was told that I had enough ammunition for about fifteen minutes. This reinforced my pessimism that this was a lost cause before the battle had even started. The Marines were assured that the Middleside Barracks (also known as "The Mile-Long Barracks") were bombproof and that the island was impregnable. When the bombing began on Corregidor on December 29, 1941, the barracks exploded, and the hospital was damaged. Two more air raids struck in January 1942.

One hundred and fifty men were in my company that set up at Battery Point. It soon became "Battered Point." The artillery could only fire in one direction because the guns had been established to protect Manila, not Corregidor. We heard rumors that the Army Air Corps planes had been caught and destroyed at Clark Field, so we only had three P-40s to fight against the invading Japanese. Just imagine this. The best and only plane we could send against the top Japanese fighters was a floatplane. We knew that defeat would be the outcome, but we continued to fight. Since I was one of the more experienced Marines at twenty-four years old, I tried to reassure the recruits by sending one or two to a cliff overlooking the South China Sea to spot any reinforcements. Of course, the South China Sea is between the Philippines and the Asian mainland. No help would be coming from that direction, but it gave the frightened young recruits some hope.

The American strategy in the Philippines was set before hostilities began. The American military policy on defense of the Philippines had changed while the islands were a Commonwealth. When we began our control of the Philippines in the early 1900s, the military decided that it would be impossible to stop an invasion. The plan was to hold Bataan and Corregidor until help arrived, and it was estimated that Bataan could resist for around two months. This decision was reaffirmed in 1937 when the Japanese invaded China. However, right before the war began, the introduction of the Boeing B-17 Flying Fortresses led the military leaders to believe that a Filipino invasion could be defeated. However, our planes were destroyed while on the ground early in the invasion of the Philippines.

The problem was that we had not updated our weapons and that the Japanese forces were vastly superior in force and in their equipment. We were using old water-cooled weapons. Most American planes had been destroyed at Pearl Harbor, and the Japanese were conquering the Philippines.

MacArthur left his headquarters and his Manila Hotel penthouse suite on December 24, 1941, and established his new headquarters in Malinta Tunnel on Corregidor. He had his wife, son, and the son's amah with him, (an amah is an Asian nanny).

As it became evident that no reinforcements would be arriving at Corregidor, rations were cut. Even if rationed, the food supply would run out by June 1942. We were allotted thirty ounces of food per day (for comparison, a large McDonald's vanilla shake is twenty-two ounces). Our ration contained eight ounces of meat (a Big Mac has 7.4 ounces), seven ounces of flour, four of beans and cereals, two ounces of rice, and three ounces of milk. Canned water was provided twice a day, and cracked wheat and syrup were extra calories. Our vision was affected by the lack of vitamins, and it was especially difficult to see at night.

We were so isolated. Bataan and Corregidor—mere specks on the map of the world stood alone against the Japanese invaders. The proverbial dominoes were falling in Asia. Subic Bay, Nichols Field, Clark Field, Cavite, and Manila had quickly been taken over by the Imperial Japanese forces. What was left of the American Asiatic Fleet was staying south of the Philippines. When Singapore fell on February 15, 1942, we knew our fate. We were next. The Japanese also quickly conquered Thailand, French Indochina, Guam, Wake, Hong Kong, Burma, and Java in addition to the large area of China that the Japanese had occupied since the 1930s.

This situation that I found myself in was this: The Philippines were being rocked under the shock of the invading Japanese. The Islands were isolated, being unmercifully attacked by the enemy forces. We just had to wait it out to see what the ending would be.

The Fourth Marines had been brought under MacArthur's command. Soon, we had to move from the remaining barracks to field positions due to the increasing air raids. The Marines on Corregidor and at nearby Fort Hughes and Fort Drum constructed landing obstacles and prepared for the inevitable invasion. Our defenses weren't much— just outdated weapons and a variety of random weapons. We were supposed to stop the Japanese at the water's edge with that equipment. Our forces prepared for invasion as well as we could with the limited artillery and weapons. Although the island was being shelled and had an occasional air raid, the brunt of the action was two miles across the water on the Bataan Peninsula. We could hear the constant artillery.

The Japanese had heard that MacArthur was on Corregidor and was planning to leave the island. FDR (President Roosevelt) had ordered him to escape to a secure location due to the concern that the general would be captured if there were a surrender. MacArthur did depart from Corregidor's North Dock on the night of March 11, 1942. He and his family, including his son's amah, and several high-ranking military members were with him as the PT boat departed. The group reached Mindanao two days later and then flew to Australia where MacArthur remained until the invasion of the Philippines began more than two years later. Many troops felt betrayed by MacArthur's departure, and I share those feelings. He left behind 90,000 troops at Bataan and Corregidor. About two-thirds of us survived the war. The last submarine left Corregidor on May 3, 1942, three days before the surrender. The word got around that there were twenty-five on board including thirteen women who were rumored to be the girlfriends of the departing soldiers. After the sub left, the mood on the island must have been like when the last lifeboat left the *Titanic.* We were just waiting for our fate. "Dugout Doug" was safe in Australia, and his men were being defeated.

Chapter Six

Surviving the Dartboard

"It was disturbing to see the Stars and Stripes lowered at Corregidor by guys with long rifles made much longer with bayonets attached. I just had to believe that this nightmare would end and that the United States military would eventually succeed."

George Burlage

Corregidor was planned and constructed in the early 1900s as a defense for Manila Bay. Coastal artillery was installed, and the facility was formally named Fort Mills. Malinta Tunnel was completed in the 1930s and included a hospital with one thousand beds, a personal bunker, and bomb proof shelters. Thirty-seven lateral tunnels extended from the main tunnel. A trolley system connected the many structures on the island.

The troops were housed in what was known as the Mile-Long Barracks. The structure was built to be hurricane proof, but the men soon learned that the barracks were not bomb proof. The barracks were destroyed in the early bombing of Corregidor, and the men started sleeping outside. When the constant bombardment of the island began after Bataan was surrendered, sleep was impossible due to the relentless shelling.

The men defending Corregidor were quickly running out of ammunition and food. They knew that there would be no reinforcements. They had been abandoned.

I did manage to send a telegram to my parents. My mother kept all the telegrams and gave them to me after the war. This telegram stated, "I am all right." My sister Lois received a letter in early May that I had mailed in late April with "no stamps available" written on the envelope's front. My parents weren't sure if I was at Bataan and truly had no idea where I was in the Philippines. By this time, we had accepted that we would not be receiving any reinforcements. I began to wonder if there was still an American military or Navy left after Pearl Harbor. They certainly weren't helping us.

Bataan surrendered on April 9, 1942, and the Japanese turned their entire energy and forces on Corregidor. A few Bataan defenders managed to cross the two miles of water to Corregidor and shared what had happened. I have a vivid memory of the strong earthquake that hit Bataan and Corregidor on April 8. I remember the date because it was the day after my 24th birthday. Adding to the noise of the earthquake, we could hear the Americans blowing up ammunition dumps across the water on Bataan. The defenders knew that the end of their battle was near. The men on Corregidor did not shell Bataan out of fear of injuring or killing the defenders. We knew that we were next. We waited and prepared as best we could with limited ammunition and supplies. We had never been issued combat gear and were still fighting in our khakis and dress shoes.

I learned after the war that General Homma (the head of Japanese forces on Bataan) had been angry that Corregidor had not been included in the Bataan surrender. He must have been very angry because he turned his weapons on Bataan toward Corregidor, and continuous attacks began. We had had few attacks until Bataan fell, but the Japanese made up for the previous lack of attention towards us. It was pure murder after Bataan surrendered. I decided that the Japanese must have captured every American artillery piece, lined them all up facing Corregidor, and started firing at us. We didn't have enough supplies to match what was being thrown at us from across the bay. The bombardment was relentless, and the ground endlessly shook. The air attacks intensified our plight, and the final seventy-two hours before the final Japanese attack and invasion were nonstop bombing and shelling. Not only did we not have enough ammunition, much of our weapons supply manufactured in the early 1930s had been affected by the tropical humidity. Less than half of our ammunition was effective. We continued to defend ourselves, but the conditions were becoming unbearable.

My assigned location was a 75-millimeter gun emplacement, and I set up my machine gun there. The emplacement had been constructed in World War I. Right behind me was a small underground ammunition storage house that offered good protection. When I would see that the artillery barrages were headed in my direction, I got into that underground area. I could hear the explosives—whomp, whomp, whomp. During one attack, I told my gunners to get into the hole with me. The hole had an iron door about a half inch thick. When the mortar hit, the door was wadded up like a sheet of paper and tossed back, knocking out all three of us. Anything that was out in the open didn't survive. The artillery continued, day and night. We had no electricity, power, or running water, and the whole island was a shroud of black. The artillery was so ferocious that metal blast doors were blown off hinges. One blast killed the man on either side of me, but I was unhurt. I didn't understand that at all, so I guess I was just lucky.

We were now on starvation rations and because of the scarcity of vitamins, our night vision was severely impaired. We were under constant attack and were sitting in the middle of a bull's eye on a small island in the huge Pacific Ocean. Our men were not prepared for any kind of sustained battle because of the lack of supplies, but we were very heavy on training and indoctrination. What supplies we did have were mostly destroyed by the bombings or were ineffective. Even the defensive guns on Corregidor that were manufactured during the Spanish Colonial Era in 1878-1888 were limited in use because they were not designed for short range attacks. They were designed to defend Manila Bay. We were in point blank range of the Japanese and really had few ways to fight back.

The forces on Corregidor knew our fate. We had gone through the stages of grief—the denial that we were in a hopeless situation (hey, we were mighty Americans!); anger that we were receiving no help at all from the American military; bargaining that if we did receive help, we could win; depression when we realized what was going to happen (defeat); and acceptance that we couldn't change what was to happen. That final acceptance was the realization that eventually we would have to surrender. A general feeling of abandonment had set in, and we were just waiting for the conclusion.

It had been drilled into our minds during boot camp that Marines did not surrender. The Marines, Semper Fi, First to Fight—all of that was the mystique of the United States Marine Corps. We didn't know if we would be ordered to fight until death or if we would fight until surrender. We just knew that the chances of defeating an invasion were practically none. The not-knowing was the worst. I learned much later that our forces numbered about 13,000. The Japanese invasion forces topped off at 75,000.

And so, we waited until the final invasion while enduring constant artillery and bombing. The days of waiting were anxious. We were so hungry. My gunner decided to head down to the depot to search for food. All he found was a gallon of minced meat, but we ate up, resulting in severe heartburn. Still, whatever we could find, we ate. We tried to stay hopeful, and we talked of going home and what we would do when we returned. Since the shelling was endless, we kept popping in and out of foxholes, wondering when the final bombardment would happen. An estimated 16,000 Japanese shells hit Corregidor on May 4 alone. I remember assessing my situation. When we had arrived on Corregidor in the early winter of 1942, the island was beautiful and full of trees. By May, there were no trees left, not even a stump. The island was bare, and in the morning light we were exposed. Japanese artillery spotter planes flew overhead, and we scrambled for cover. We were so weary and just wanted the inevitable invasion to happen. It was a strange feeling to anticipate an attack that we knew we could not defeat. Many of the officers thought that the Japanese would invade at sunrise. They thought wrong.

The actual final assault was quite late at night on May 5, 1942. The Allied forces had held back the Japanese for more than three weeks. We were a hungry group of Marines, run down by malnutrition and short on weapons, but we fought the attackers. We could hear the engines and firing down the beach from Battery Point. I was overlooking the beach where I could see a bit of what was happening and got into some of the sniper fire. It was dark, pitch dark—no moon, no stars, just dark. Small arms fire met the landing forces, but coastal artillery fire was useless because of the closeness of the final fight. The Fourth Marines fought hard, but our old World War I -style grenades were no match against the superior Japanese knee mortars (very effective and quick grenade launchers), and also, the Japanese had several regiments of reinforcements and had landed their tanks. We had no defense against the tanks. None of our weapons could penetrate the tanks' armor. I had been issued six thousand rounds of ammunition for my machine gun. My sergeant had estimated that small amount of ammunition would last for fifteen minutes, so I attempted to ration the bullets.

The heavy artillery did not let up. I had been fighting all night and must have fallen asleep due to exhaustion and being on edge for so long. It was daylight when I woke up. The fighting was still in full force, but I was too far away to do much. The battle had moved down the beach from where I was, and I was watching and waiting. Suddenly, my company commander came over and said, "Don't fire. It's over." I didn't know whether to believe him or not, and then he sent a runner who instructed us not to destroy our weapons because the surrender would be unconditional. Too late. I had already destroyed my rifle, taking it apart piece by piece and throwing the pieces into the South China Sea. The rifle was special to me as I had had it since boot camp. I loved that rifle. It had served me well, and I didn't want to see it in enemy hands. My rifle was my friend, and I still remember the serial number—988186. I had just finished getting rid of my rifle when a Japanese soldier came over and ordered us to stay where we were. We were surrounded, and we knew that it was over. He told us in English, "You can't leave. Stay here."

After a twelve-hour battle that resulted in 800 Allied troops killed, with one thousand wounded, and 900 Japanese deaths, General Jonathan Wainwright (known as "Skinny" to his men) sent a message to President Roosevelt on May 6. This message was "there is a limit of human endurance, and that point has long been passed." The Fourth Marine Regiment's flag was burned, and Wainwright surrendered the Corregidor garrison on May 6, 1942, at 1:30 p.m. Do I remember this date? A man doesn't forget the worst day of his life. My ATM code is 5642. The Imperial Japanese Forces now controlled the Philippines and most of Asia. The plan had been to conquer the Philippines in two months, but it required four months instead. That pushed back the Japanese military plan to invade Hawaii, so I guess we accomplished something.

A few hours later, some Marines sitting on the roadside lit up cigarettes, and all hell broke loose. The Japanese opened fire on them, but no one was hurt. The next morning, a Japanese platoon came to round us up and marched us to a central location. I didn't know what to expect. We had been told that the Japanese would not take prisoners, and one of the old Corps types told me to save my last bullet for myself because we would be tortured. I was so tired and so numb that I didn't really care at that moment.

The Fourth Marines adopted a motto after Corregidor— "Surrendered, yes. Defeated, never." We knew that there was no choice but to surrender, but we were surrendered as a group by our commanders. There was no individual surrendering. One thousand, four hundred and eighty-seven Fourth Marines were captured at Corregidor. One-third of these men (474) died before the war ended. Between April 9 and May 6, 1942, the Japanese had captured 20,000 Americans and 68,000 Filipinos at Bataan and Corregidor. The estimated deaths from the Bataan Death March were in the thousands.

When we were surrendered, we soon realized that the Japanese weren't at all organized to take care of captives. They had little structure, relying on a beating or a bayonet. The officers had samurai swords. How we survived those first few days of captivity is a miracle, but we found the will to live was very strong. The Japanese had not expected such a large surrender and truly did not seem to know what to do with us. We sat in the hot tropical sun with no water nor instructions for days. We also soon learned we had but one chance of survival— work for the Emperor's war effort. Forty months of slave labor was our future.

Homefront

The news of Corregidor's surrender reached the United States quickly. *The Visalia Times-Delta* newspaper in George Burlage's hometown included two articles soon after the surrender. On May 8, 1942, a short news item was in the newspaper:

Mr. and Mrs. George S. Burlage of the Ivanhoe District have received word from the War Department to the effect that their son, George E. Burlage, in the Philippine Islands has been listed as missing.

Two weeks later, another article was printed in the Visalia newspaper.

Mother's Day held tragic significances to many mothers in this bruised and baffled world. It was estimated that last Sunday, there were more sons away from their mothers than at any time in U.S. history since 1918 when the A.E.F. was in France and preparing to go "over there."

Perhaps some of you recall the cheery letter written by George E. Burlage, son of Mr. and Mrs. George S. Burlage of Ivanhoe District to his sister. It appeared in March in "the Times- Delta." It came

from the Bataan area. Since then, Bataan and Corregidor have fallen. Mrs. Burlage knew, on Mother's Day last, that her son, the Leatherneck young Marine who had written home the words, "Don't worry about me!" had been officially listed as missing. Thus passed Mother's Day 1942 for George's mother.

George and Rebecca Burlage received a telegram on May 8 confirming that their son was listed as missing in the Philippines. The MIA status would remain for more than a year.

Chapter Seven

After Surrender

"The loss of freedom was abrupt. I decided quickly that although my body had been captured, my mind was still free.

"No one could capture my mind."

George Burlage

The afternoon of May 6, 1942, George Burlage and the other 11,000 new prisoners-of-war who had been captured on Corregidor sat in the tropical sun in what was known as the 92nd Garage, a beach area that had been used to store vehicles. No water, food, or shelter had been provided. The Japanese guards had given few instructions to the men, and the new prisoners had no idea what would happen next. The new prisoners soon realized how captivity would be—brutal and uncompassionate.

That's when George Burlage swore a silent oath to himself that he would survive whatever was in his future. He had ambitions and plans for his life, and no one was taking that away from him.

He immediately joined a work detail, stole a guard's canteen, and planned how he would one day be free. He would not give up.

I lost my freedom when Corregidor was surrendered. I nor any of the men who had been captured knew what to expect as a prisoner-of-war. There had been no choice but to surrender as we were out of ammunition and supplies. Our surrender did not give us POW status, and we did not have to be treated by the rules of the Geneva Convention regarding humane treatment of POWs because the Japanese government had not agreed to its laws. The Japanese military had refused to grant prisoner-of-war status to those captured at Bataan because the Japanese hierarchy was angry that Wainwright had not surrendered Corregidor when Bataan fell. As bad as our treatment was, it was nothing like the Bataan POWs experienced.

I soon learned that POW survival would be by wit, luck, and being in the right place by the right time. Any sickness could be fatal due to the lack of medicine, food, and sanitation. We were in total blackout for forty months. We had no idea what was happening with the war or even if the war was still going on. Often, our guards told us about events and victories that never happened. We never witnessed any battles after Corregidor until the Americans invaded in 1944 and we saw the bombers coming in. We were totally isolated from the rest of the world. The only true news that we received was when Roosevelt died. A guard told us, "Roosevelt, that son-of-a-bitch, is dead. Japan will win the war now." Of course, only the first part of that was true.

When I was on the *Leatherneck* magazine staff (the official USMC magazine) in the 1950s, I wrote a series of articles about my prisoner-of-war experiences. This is how I described my capture:

The white flag was up, all weapons that could be were destroyed. The afternoon of May 6, 1942, the remaining men of the USAFFE would cease to exist as a fighting unit.

The Japanese were moving in all over the island of Corregidor, and the isolated packets of men were being rounded up. There was still firing upon the island at intervals. That night we considered sleeping but were awakened when several batteries of artillery opened up on our group from the Bataan shore. Heavy shelling lasted for several minutes and then suddenly stopped.

At daybreak the following morning, we were moved out of the sector that we had tried to defend. Along the route of the march – there were but a few hundred of us in our group – there was sporadic artillery fire from Bataan, and an occasional dive bomber would drop light bombs. Our guard seemed as surprised as we were about the attacks.

We were herded together on Topside in the sun (May is the hottest month in the Philippines). The Japanese soldiers didn't know what to do with us, and their lack of training was evident. We had no food or water that day.

That night, we were moved up to the opposite side of the island. The Japanese had buried their dead but had left the Americans where they had fallen. An estimated 11,000 Americans and Filipinos were crowded onto the beach with no shade. This area was known as "the 92nd Area Garage." It was where the 92nd Coast artillery vehicles had been parked. No drinking water was provided for three days, and after a conduit from water reserves was installed, the men had to stand for hours to fill canteens. The guards took personal possessions from the captives, and severe punishment resulted if any "Made in Japan" items or Japanese currency was found on a prisoner. After the war, I was told that Bataan prisoners were executed if any "Made in Japan" personal possessions were discovered while being searched.

Due to thirst, heat exhaustion, malaria, and dysentery, the death rate rose. Some form of cleanliness and sanitation was practiced, but only the most primitive methods could be used. Pits were dug on hillsides for latrines, but they soon overflowed into the crowded 92nd Garage area. The men stole or looted food when they could and were told by their guards that all remaining food supplies were now Japanese property. The area was quickly christened "Dysentery Flats."

The Japanese divided us into groups of approximately 1,000 men each with American colonels in charge of the groups. There was also an imaginary line between the Filipino captives and the Americans. No one crossed that line in fear of being shot. We were given a number by the Japanese, and it was ordered that the number be painted on the back of our shirts. I was now renamed "Kyu-ju go," number ninety-five in Japanese. During morning roll call, I was not George Burlage but just a number, and I answered to that number for forty months. Everything was taken from us—watches, rings, wallets, and money. Any of us who had Japanese items with us quickly disposed of them as we had heard that we would be shot if we were discovered with those items on us. We were also instructed, really ordered, to bow to and salute any Japanese.

Standing on that beach after our surrender, I assessed the situation in the 92nd Garage. I witnessed men sitting on the ground, moaning, "We're not going to make it. We're done for." I gave this attitude a name—"give up-itis." Looking at the thousands of prisoners, many who I realize weren't mentally strong enough to survive whatever might be ahead of us, I made a pledge to myself that I would survive and that "no damn Japanese is going to kill me."

I soon realized that I had to become smarter than the enemy to survive. As a group of us was being moved from our defensive positions to a holding area, a Japanese soldier pulled me out of the column, kicked me, and grunted for me to push a stalled truck up the hill. I was choking for water and becoming desperate. Taking in the situation, I saw the soldier's canteen on the truck seat. I pointed to the brake drum which was burning and as the soldier looked at the drum, both I and his canteen disappeared into the column. That was my confidence I needed to see me through. I now knew that I could outsmart them.

There was a mental transition to becoming a prisoner-of-war. Your status and well-being changes abruptly. Mentally, you are ashamed for failing. Add the physical maltreatment— beatings, starvation, being worked to physical exhaustion, and staying alive only by luck or wit. After the war, it was revealed by the War Department (now Department of Defense) that only 45 percent of Americans captured by the Japanese survived compared to 97 percent of those who were German prisoners. Survival was truly a battle of will.

It soon became apparent that working would provide food. I joined a work detail on Corregidor after I watched the sergeant who had recruited me in Los Angeles die. After I joined a cleanup/burial detail, I had food and water. I also joined work details that were assigned with cleaning up the island and gathering ammunition and food for the Japanese to transport to Manila. Men were beaten for stealing food. We were told that everything on Corregidor now belonged to the Japanese government.

After enduring three days without water, we were finally allowed to install a small pipe as a conduit from water reserves two miles away. Men stood in line for four to six hours just to fill one canteen with water. There were swarms of flies around the open latrines. Dysentery, heat strokes, malaria, and malnutrition weakened and killed the prisoners.

We had a talkative Japanese corporal for our guard, and he let us eat whatever we could find. He also told us that he was about to join a unit preparing to invade Australia. According to him, after the capture of Australia, the Japanese military would go to Hawaii, occupy the islands and eat pineapples, then go on to California and eventually capture President Roosevelt and dictate surrender terms at the White House. "Then," the corporal added, "Japan will defeat Germany, who is our real enemy, and we will rule the world." After what we had witnessed at Bataan and Corregidor, few of us doubted that a Japanese conquest could happen.

In the first weeks of captivity, 2,800 Americans and 27,000 Filipinos died. These numbers increased steadily before liberation forty months later. Even if I had known my chances of surviving prison camp, I would have still sworn that I would make it.

RETURNING TO CORREGIDOR

In 1952, while serving as a combat correspondent for *Leatherneck* magazine during the Korean conflict, I was assigned to travel to Corregidor to write about my war experiences. This article was published in *Leatherneck* in 1952. These were my reactions when I went back ten years after the battle. I was surprised and disappointed that there had been no attempt to beautify the island. Nothing much had changed since I had last seen Corregidor in 1942.

From Corregidor: 10 years later
By Msgt. George Burlage, USMC

Ten years (after I had departed the island), as the boat in which I was riding approached Corregidor, these events of the decade before whirled through my memory, and I relived the days of withdrawals, siege, and final surrender. The boat came out of Manila Bay and headed into the North Channel to make the North dock of Corregidor. To the right was the tip of Bataan from where the Japanese had launched their final and successful assault against the island, and just to my left was Monkey Point where their successful landing took place (the name was derived decades before due to the large number of monkeys that lived there). I leaned upon the gunwales to get a closer view of the landing spot now covered with the green of tropical vegetation. What a contrast to the brown, dusty, and treeless island the Japanese had laid bare and beaten into submission by bomb and shell.

Momentarily, the green serenity of Monkey Point faded and reverted to the brown and battered strip of land of that fateful noonday hour on May 6, 1942. At this hour, that shell marked point, and the rest of Corregidor passed from a besieged but free land to the control of the Japanese Army. The hot noonday sun had beaten down upon the narrow beach off the point where flies and the smell of death had grown stronger with the rising sun. Japanese landing boats, damaged in the landing, littered the beach, and the scattered lifejackets of their occupants bore grim testimony of what had transpired the night before. Men of the Fourth Marines, poorly equipped and hungry, had accounted well for themselves that night as they held off the first of two landings with their Springfield rifles, a couple of Lewis guns, and a few water cooled 30's. Their mission was a sacrifice that seemed almost in vain next morning with the Army commander's decision to surrender.

The jolt of the boat as it bumped against the dock brought me back to reality. It was the same dock that we Fourth Marines had used when we came from Bataan during the early days of fighting. Once the busiest spot on the island, especially during the first months of the war when troops and supplies were being evacuated from the mainland, the dock was now deserted and partially destroyed. A heavy bomb or shell had struck near its center and had chipped and cracked the concrete structure; these broken pieces were still held together with steel reinforcing rods which clung to them in a tired pose as the dock bent downward towards the water.

Since the end of World War II, rumors have been circulated in the States that the Filipinos had converted Corregidor into a national shrine to commemorate their fight for independence and as a monument to those men who futilely defended their freedom against the Japanese and later re-won it during the War of Philippine Liberation. This is far from the truth. The debris of war, although partially hidden by the grass and vegetation of a long-deserted area, still covers the island. The only signs of life were at Bottomside where a few Filipino soldiers maintained a small ammunition dump at Malinta tunnel and lived with their families in a group of huts near the tunnel's entrance. Around the area, postwar children played in the ruins of war unmindful of the historic and at one time grim past of their playground.

It was with great interest that I returned to Corregidor. I had done guard duty here at the Navy Radio Tunnel when it was first established in 1940 and then after the start of the war, my company (Fourth Marines) took up their beach defense positions here. With prewar and wartime experiences and memories of Corregidor, it was only natural to want to see the place again. My first wish was to go to the eastern end of the island to see the area from the land that I had earlier seen from the bay. A Filipino officer offered the loan of the only truck on the island but at first refused to allow the driver to go through Malinta Tunnel or out to this section of the island.

The officer had argued that the tunnel was dark and dangerous while the area beyond that was inhabited by poisonous snakes. It appeared that he was right on both counts. The noise of the truck echoed through the cold stillness of the tunnel as the driver groped his way in the semi darkness. Here and there a scar in the hard surface of the roadbed, which was caused by heavy explosion, or a boarded-up entrance to one of the laterals bore evidence of fighting done by those who had come later to liberate the Philippines. Everywhere was the mute testimony of the history and tragedies of the war that had happened here – decisions by MacArthur, of Wainwright, of a quartermaster officer attempting to hoard his dwindling supplies, and of doctors and the dying in the hospital laterals.

As the truck came out of the east end of the tunnel, the road ceased to exist. Ahead where the road and streetcar tracks once were, there was only a wall of grass and trees. Scars of war – the shell craters and an earth beaten brown and stripped of all plant life – were gone. In their place was only the placid green of an unmolested jungle. A narrow strip of grass that grew up to the height of 8 feet ran through the jungle with vigorous young trees crowding up to its edge. This had been the road, the ground still too wrecked from wartime usage for the larger plants and trees to grow.

The driver fought his way through the grass and stayed on the old roadbed mainly because he could not leave it through the thick wall of trees that lined its sides. Every landmark was gone. The grass and trees had erased them in their growth. The airstrip had disappeared long ago under its layer of tropical growth, and the cemetery had suffered a similar fate.

Farther to the east, four wooden poles loomed forlornly out of the tall grass; these were the only reminder of what had once been installations of the Navy Radio Tunnel that occupied the area. The 92nd Garage, known as "Dysentery Flats," to the thousands who were herded into its cramped area by the Japanese, was inaccessible. From a distance, the red rust of the naked iron beams of the building that had long ago lost its covering of corrugated tin glowed in sharp contrast against the tropical green to form a decaying memorial to those who suffered, lived, and died within its enclosure.

Back at Bottomside, there was but one road to take to see the remaining accessible parts of the island. The roads that once supplied the former Marine positions at Battery Point, James Ravine, and the southern shore of Corregidor were closed and overgrown with vegetation. Only the main road to Topside was still open, and this was only wide enough for one-way traffic to the lighthouse that overlooks the China Sea.

Halfway up the hill are the remains of Middleside. Here are the ruins of the mile-long barracks, once officially declared to be "bombproof" but proven otherwise after the first concentrated bombings on the island. Marines moving on to Corregidor were caught in the first daylight raid on the area and were ordered to take shelter in these barracks. While the Marines huddled on the first floor, the Japanese dive bombers blew off the roof and parts of the top floor. The barracks remain much in the same condition today with fat lizards sunning themselves in the debris of destruction. On the south, an unnamed jungle vine climbs the reinforced corner to the full height of the original building and accentuates the deserted stillness with its fiery red blossoms.

On up the road leading to Topside are the once powerful land batteries of long barreled coastal rifles that pointed only seaward and the snubbed nosed mortars and howitzers that were used for closer targets. Unlike other parts of the island, here concrete aprons prevent the vegetation from taking over and covering these batteries. The guns, although nearly three quarters of a century old, still carry a symbol of power. Battery Way, the former 12-inch howitzer battery, is typical of this pose, the guns remaining in a firing position with their barrels pointing belligerently skyward.

I climbed the rest of the way to the top to see the parade ground, but this, too, was hidden under feet of vegetation. The only landmark was the flagpole with its lower half surrounded by trees and jungle vegetation. At intervals, through a break in the vegetation, gutted buildings could be seen. As nothing seemed the same, I paused to get my directions and then continued to the lighthouse. A new one had replaced the one that was damaged by the Japanese, and I climbed the stairs to the lookout tower so I could get an unrestricted view of the surrounding land and sea.

Behind me was the China Sea and as I faced towards the east, I saw the city of Manila outline 30 miles away. Below me the tadpole -shaped island looked placidly green in the mid-afternoon sun. Off to the right lay Caballo Island, equally as beautiful; farther to the right was Fort Drum, now gutted and discarded; and finally, Fort Frank, belonging more to the Batangas shoreline then to the chain of forts that once guarded Manila Bay.

I then gazed northward across the three-mile channel to this shore of Bataan into the cloud that always covers the peak of Mount Mariveles. Then my gaze finally wandered back to the flagpole. This was the same pole from which the American flag once flew so proudly and defiantly. This pole, although bare and half covered with jungle vegetation, still carried a symbol of achievement and pride which is understood by all Americans. As I continued to gaze, I thought of the past, of the future, and of legends already starting about the American and Filipino brotherhood of arms. The one that stood out in my mind that afternoon was the story of the lowering of the flag from the flagpole and of the Marine that carried it, wrapped around his body, to the prison camp of Cabanatuan.

I looked again on the ruins and stillness of Corregidor. A decade ago, men fought for freedom and an ideal on this island, and the word "Corregidor" was a proud symbol to the people of the free world. Now, in another age of science and social advancement— and of war— the island of Corregidor had been abandoned and forgotten. Other "corregidors" have been discarded along the way, to be remembered only by those who participated in their struggles. Like the men who fight, these places have died and have been forgotten, but that freedom and the American ideals for which they fought will live forever. Corregidor is gone, but the spirit of those who suffered there will never die. It will live as in the legend of the American flag.

(Corregidor is now restored. The bombed-out barracks, cinema, and other buildings have been reinforced but are shells. The Pacific War

Museum is housed on the island, and visitors can visit Battery Point and other important sites in Corregidor's history.)

Chapter Eight

Manila to Cabanatuan

"How we survived those first days of captivity is somewhat of a miracle, but we found the will to live to be strong. We soon realized we had one choice toward survival—work for the emperor's war effort."

George Burlage

The prisoners were kept on Corregidor until the Japanese decided how to handle the thousands of captives. In late May 1942, the prisoners were taken by boats to Manila and after disembarking, were marched through the streets to Bilibid Prison in the city, a jail that had been built during the Spanish colonial period. The Japanese Victory parade featured the conquering General Homma, the Corregidor POWs, and confiscated American weapons. The Japanese used Bilibid as a makeshift hospital and as a holding pen while the prisoners' camps were being assigned.

Soon George Burlage was transferred to Cabanatuan. The camp had been a training facility for the Philippine Army and was overcrowded and disease-ridden. He and the other prisoners were transported to the Cabanatuan area in narrow gauge boxcars and then marched to the camp from the nearby train station. As

George saw his new "home," he began looking for a way to get out of the camp.

Our return to Manila was under a different setting than when we had last seen it in the closing days of 1941. Four thousand Corregidor prisoners were transferred to Manila on May 24. It was a totally humiliating experience for the American prisoners.

Three Japanese transports sat off in Corregidor's South Channel; this was our transportation to the mainland. The ships finished loading by dark and remained moored until the next morning when the ships made the thirty-one-mile voyage across Manila Bay. Midmorning, the ships dropped anchor in the south part of the bay off Paranaque, and we disembarked in landing boats. In waist-deep water, the boats turned back and stopped, and we jumped out and waded to the shore. Wading ashore, we found a troop of Japanese soldiers waiting for us to continue our march. Assembling the prisoners into groups, the Japanese started us towards the main part of Manila via Dewey Boulevard. It would have been much simpler to have taken us to the port area, but their reasons for this route beginning on the outskirts of the city were quite clear. Along the route of the march were the residences of the Spanish and White Russians of the city ("White Russians" were exiles from the 1917 Russian Revolution). The Japanese were showing off their "prizes" – captured Americans.

The march's route turned to the south of the Walled City and onto Taft Avenue, across Quezon Bridge, and out on Quezon Boulevard to the ancient and condemned Bilibid Prison. Along the route, groups of Filipinos and White Russians gathered to watch. We were a curiosity, and some were attempting to find friends and family members. The Filipinos who attempted to give the prisoners food, candy, or cigarettes were slapped or beaten by the guards. Occasionally, a Filipino would quietly flash the V for victory sign or scream out in recognition of a prisoner. Women, upon recognizing someone close to them, would become uncontrollable and rush to the street, only to be beaten or shoved by a guard. The march's purpose was to show the Filipinos that the Japanese were a superior race to the Americans.

Inside Bilibid, there was the usual confusion and disorganization that we were already accustomed to enduring. The prison was crowded with men lying and sleeping wherever they could. There were about 12,000 prisoners there in a place designed for 4,000. Food was rice and was rationed. A five-gallon gasoline barrel was filled with rice to serve fifty men.

The next morning, prisoners began to be moved. The Americans were being taken out in four different details, one per day, to Cabanatuan. Many Filipinos, weak and dying from malaria and dysentery, had to be carried out by friends as they were sent to Camp O'Donnell, the dreaded death camp where the Bataan Death March survivors were taken. The Japanese were attempting to separate the Filipinos and Americans. The American prisoners were marched to the railroad depot and were loaded one hundred to a boxcar (there were small cars from a narrow-gauge railroad) with the help of the sentries' bayonets and rifle butts. No one could sit, and we remained standing in the intense and suffocating heat for hours. I kept thinking about how long it had been since I had a shower. We had no water, no food, obviously no restrooms. The trip took most of a day and was pure misery. We disembarked at Cabanatuan, the rice center of the Philippines, and where one of the last battles of Bataan was fought. We were issued no additional clothing until we were shipped to Japan in the fall of 1944. By that time, we were working practically naked.

Staying overnight in a schoolyard with a rainstorm made the wet ground even more uncomfortable, so we were glad to get underway the next morning. We were warned as we started our twelve-mile march to our concentration camp that stragglers would be shot. We believed it. We had finally learned about what had happened on the Bataan Death March.

Illustration 1. George Burlage's third grade photo.

He attended grades one through eight at East Lynn County School near Visalia, California. He is in the second row from bottom, first on the left.

Illustration 2. Boot Camp graduation, San Diego, California.

Burlage is in the second row from the top, second left.

Illustration 3. Calesas (Kalesa—Tagalog) lined up by the Cavite Navy Yard for customers.

Burlage Archives

Illustration 4. Pfc. George Burlage enjoying the island life at Cavite.

Burlage Archives

Illustration 5. Barracks at Cavite.

Burlage Archives

Illustration 6. Cavite Town Patrol.

Burlage Archives

Their duties included breaking up bar fights and arresting drunken Marines and sailors. Burlage is top row, third from right.

Illustration 7. Advertising at Cavite.

Burlage Archives

Illustration 8. Last peacetime Christmas at Cavite Navy Yard.

Burlage Archives

Illustration 9. Cavite Navy Yard after Japanese bombings in December 1941.

www.history.navy.mil, National Archives

Illustration 10. Waterfront damage at Cavite.

www.history.navy.mil, National Archives
The base was abandoned after the attacks, and the men were sent as reinforcements to Bataan.

Illustration 11. Burlage's last telegram before leaving for Bataan.

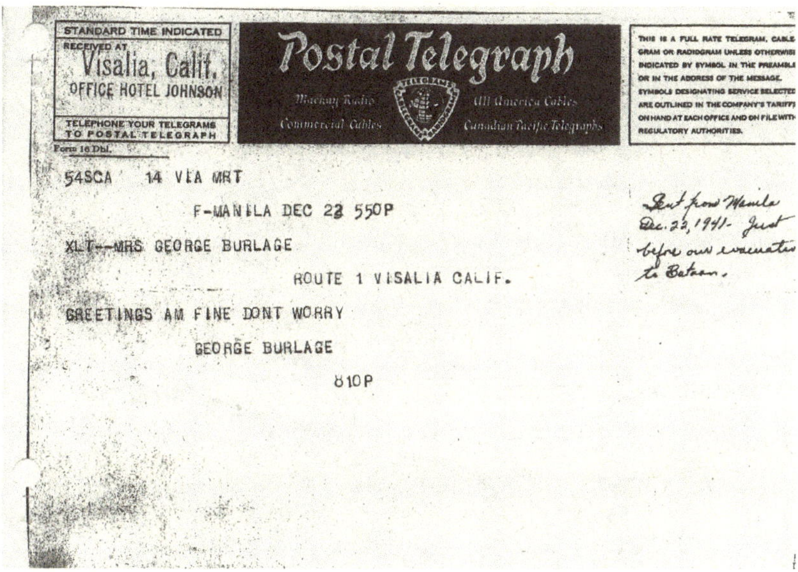

STANDARD TIME INDICATED
RECEIVED AT
Visalia, Calif.
OFFICE HOTEL JOHNSON
TELEPHONE YOUR TELEGRAMS TO POSTAL TELEGRAPH
Form 16 Dbl.

Postal Telegraph
Mackay Radio — All America Cables
Commercial Cables — Canadian Pacific Telegraphs

THIS IS A FULL RATE TELEGRAM, CABLEGRAM OR RADIOGRAM UNLESS OTHERWISE INDICATED BY SYMBOL IN THE PREAMBLE OR IN THE ADDRESS OF THE MESSAGE. SYMBOLS DESIGNATING SERVICE SELECTED ARE OUTLINED IN THE COMPANY'S TARIFFS ON HAND AT EACH OFFICE AND ON FILE WITH REGULATORY AUTHORITIES.

54SCA 14 VIA MRT
F-MANILA DEC 22 550P
XLT--MRS GEORGE BURLAGE
ROUTE 1 VISALIA CALIF.
GREETINGS AM FINE DONT WORRY
GEORGE BURLAGE
810P

Sent from Manila Dec. 22, 1941- Just before our evacuation to Bataan.

Burlage Archives

He added the written explanations when he returned home in 1945. His mother kept all correspondence, telegrams, and articles from and about her son.

Illustration 12. Map of Luzon battle area in the Philippines.

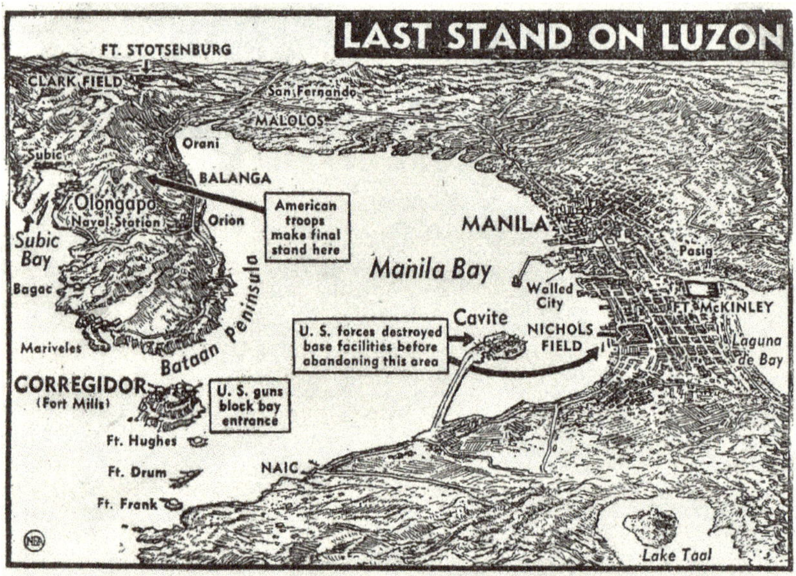

On a rugged, mountainous peninsula and a heavily fortified island American and Filipino troops are making their final stand against Japanese invaders of Luzon. Map shows the Bataan Peninsula-Corregidor-Manila area where U. S. and Jap forces clash.

Burlage Archives

Burlage's mother had saved this from their local newspaper, the *Visalia Times-Delta.*

Illustration 13. Map of Corregidor.

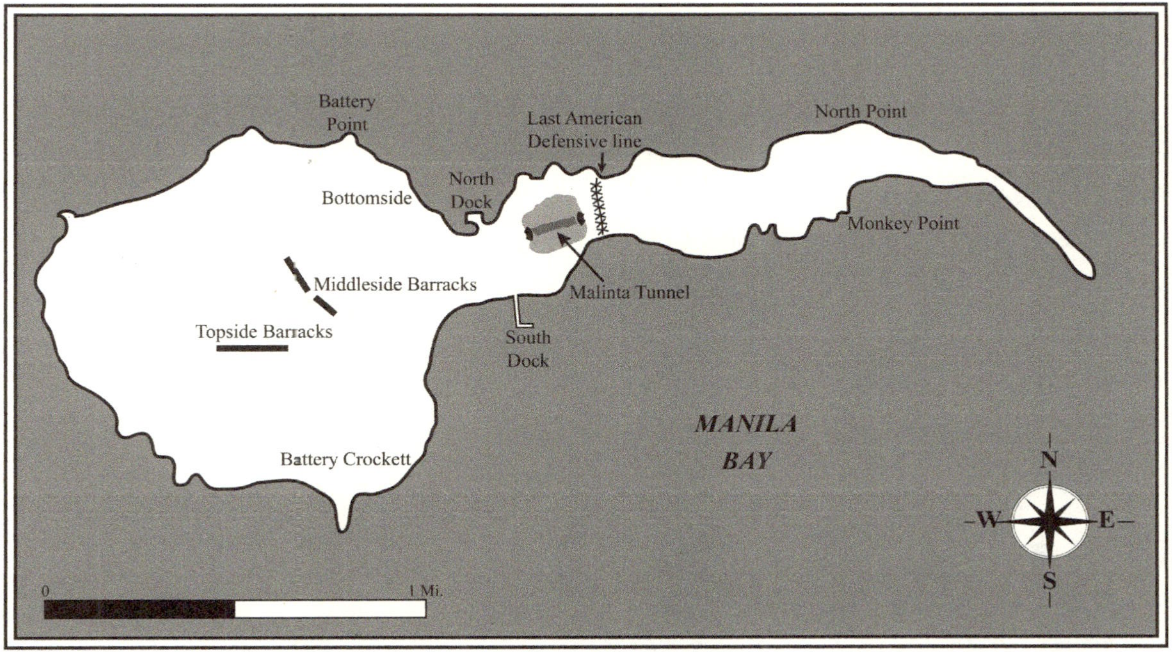

Map courtesy Alex Mendoza
Burlage was assigned to Battery Point. (www.corregidor.com)

Illustration 14. Battery Point in 1952.

Burlage Archives

Illustration 15. A view of the Mile-Long Barracks as seen across Corregidor Island in 1952.

Burlage Archives

Illustration 16. The bombed-out Mile-Long (Topside) Barracks.

Burlage Archives

The barracks were built to be hurricane-proof. The actual length of the building was one-third of a mile.

Illustration 17. Lowering the American flag on Corregidor after the May 6, 1942, surrender.

Philippine Expeditionary Force compiled by Gasei. Published by the Watdri Group Information Department, Philippines, 1943

Illustration 18. Japanese general Masahura Homma.

Philippine Expeditionary Force compiled by Gasei. Published by the Watdri Group Information Department, Philippines, 1943

General Homma was the head of the Philippine Expeditionary Force. Here, he reviews the Victory Parade in Manila in late May 1942. The prisoners who were captured at Corregidor were forced to march in the parade.

Illustration 19. Official telegram to Burlage's parents informing them of their son's prisoner-of-war status.

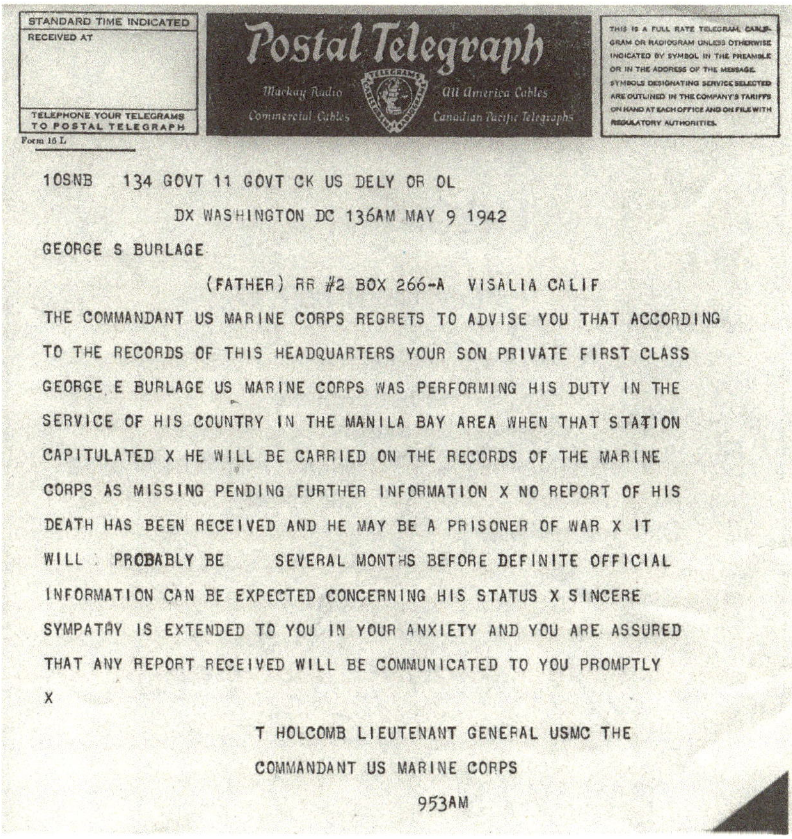

STANDARD TIME INDICATED
RECEIVED AT

TELEPHONE YOUR TELEGRAMS TO POSTAL TELEGRAPH

Form 16 L

Postal Telegraph

Mackay Radio — All America Cables — Commercial Cables — Canadian Pacific Telegraphs

THIS IS A FULL RATE TELEGRAM, CABLEGRAM OR RADIOGRAM UNLESS OTHERWISE INDICATED BY SYMBOL IN THE PREAMBLE OR IN THE ADDRESS OF THE MESSAGE. SYMBOLS DESIGNATING SERVICE SELECTED ARE OUTLINED IN THE COMPANY'S TARIFFS ON HAND AT EACH OFFICE AND ON FILE WITH REGULATORY AUTHORITIES.

1OSNB 134 GOVT 11 GOVT CK US DELY OR OL

DX WASHINGTON DC 136AM MAY 9 1942

GEORGE S BURLAGE

(FATHER) RR #2 BOX 266-A VISALIA CALIF

THE COMMANDANT US MARINE CORPS REGRETS TO ADVISE YOU THAT ACCORDING TO THE RECORDS OF THIS HEADQUARTERS YOUR SON PRIVATE FIRST CLASS GEORGE E BURLAGE US MARINE CORPS WAS PERFORMING HIS DUTY IN THE SERVICE OF HIS COUNTRY IN THE MANILA BAY AREA WHEN THAT STATION CAPITULATED X HE WILL BE CARRIED ON THE RECORDS OF THE MARINE CORPS AS MISSING PENDING FURTHER INFORMATION X NO REPORT OF HIS DEATH HAS BEEN RECEIVED AND HE MAY BE A PRISONER OF WAR X IT WILL PROBABLY BE SEVERAL MONTHS BEFORE DEFINITE OFFICIAL INFORMATION CAN BE EXPECTED CONCERNING HIS STATUS X SINCERE SYMPATHY IS EXTENDED TO YOU IN YOUR ANXIETY AND YOU ARE ASSURED THAT ANY REPORT RECEIVED WILL BE COMMUNICATED TO YOU PROMPTLY X

T HOLCOMB LIEUTENANT GENERAL USMC THE COMMANDANT US MARINE CORPS

953AM

Burlage Archives

Illustration 20. Location of prisoner-of-war camps in the Philippines.

httpy://owl.english.purdue.edu/owl/section/2/

Burlage was imprisoned at Cabanatuan, Palawan, Bilibid, and Las Pinas before being sent to Japan.

Illustration 21. 1943 article from the *Visalia Times-Delta* updating Burlage's status.

Seven-Month Silence Boken by Prisoner of War

Breaking a silence that has existed since December, 1943, is a Prisoner of War postal card message from Cpl. George E. Burlage, USMC, addressed to his sister "Miss Lois Burlage, route 2, box 890." The sister has been married since Corporal Burlage was taken prisoner at Bataan and is now Mrs. David Brase, but Corporal Burlage is probably not aware of that. He is the son of Mr. and Mrs. George R. Burlage of the Ivanhoe district.

The postal card is on a form printed by the Imperial Japanese Army. Part of it is printed out and blank spaces are left for insertions and then room is provided for a 50-word message. It informs Corporal Burlage's relatives that he is interned at Philippine Military Prison Camp No. 4. (He was formerly interned at Camp No. 10).

"My health is good. Trust all are well at home. Regards and best wishes to all. Keep your chin up and I will try to continue the same. Take care of the folks at home. Love."

Only four messages have been received from Corporal Burlage since he was taken prisoner by the Japanese.

Illustration 22. Article from the *Visalia Times-Delta*.

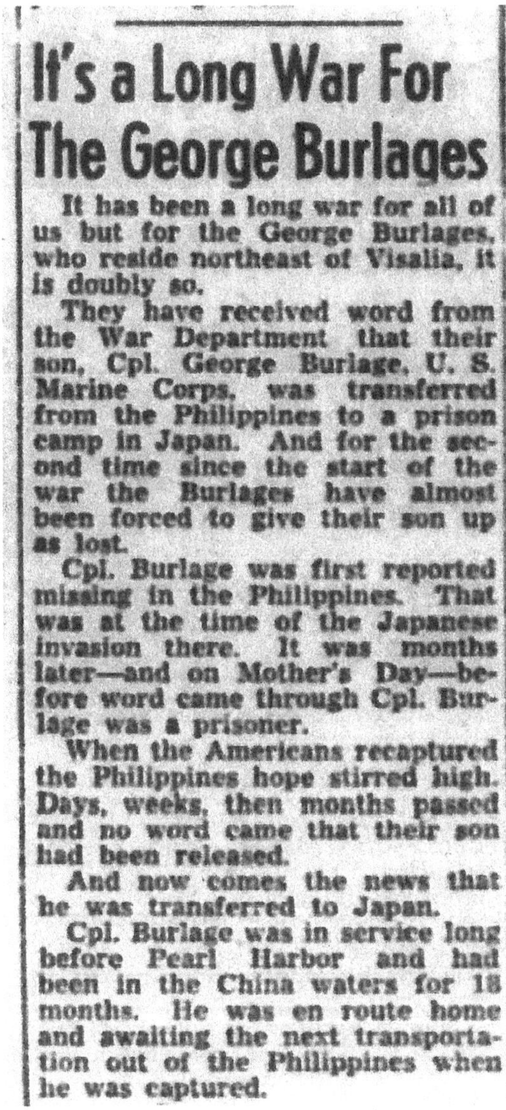

It's a Long War For The George Burlages

It has been a long war for all of us but for the George Burlages, who reside northeast of Visalia, it is doubly so.

They have received word from the War Department that their son, Cpl. George Burlage, U. S. Marine Corps, was transferred from the Philippines to a prison camp in Japan. And for the second time since the start of the war the Burlages have almost been forced to give their son up as lost.

Cpl. Burlage was first reported missing in the Philippines. That was at the time of the Japanese invasion there. It was months later—and on Mother's Day—before word came through Cpl. Burlage was a prisoner.

When the Americans recaptured the Philippines hope stirred high. Days, weeks, then months passed and no word came that their son had been released.

And now comes the news that he was transferred to Japan.

Cpl. Burlage was in service long before Pearl Harbor and had been in the China waters for 18 months. He was en route home and awaiting the next transportation out of the Philippines when he was captured.

Illustration 23. *Hokusen Maru*—Burlage's hell ship. His voyage took 38 days.

www.west-point.org

Illustration 24. Hell ship route very similar to Burlage's voyage of almost forty days.

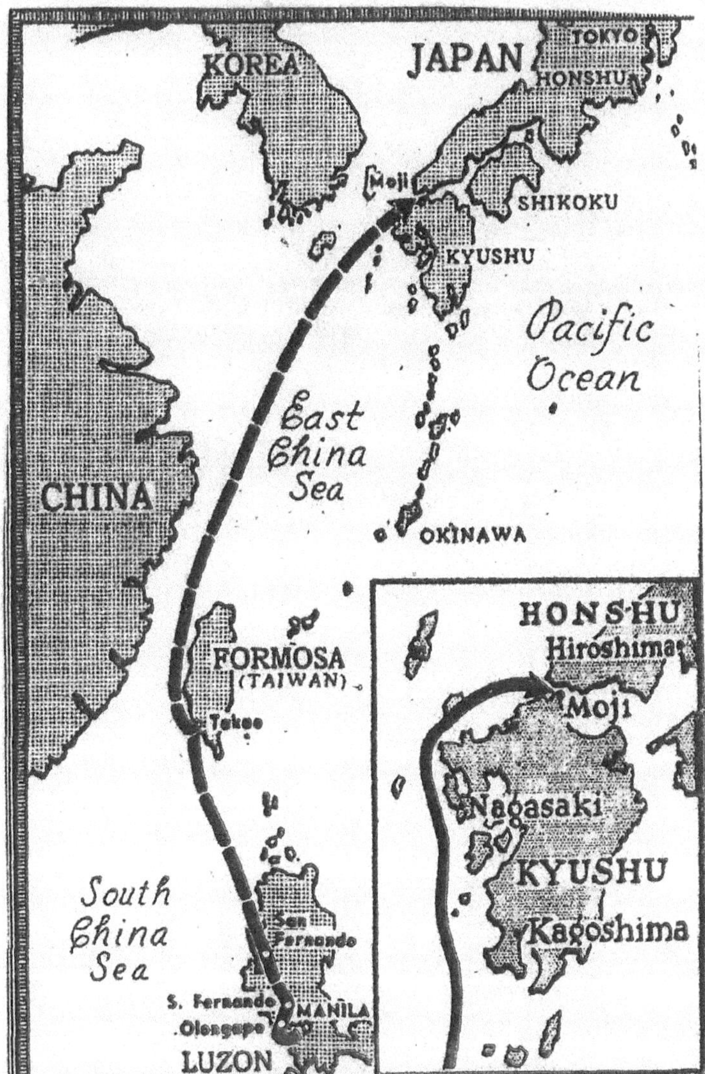

www.mansell.org

Illustration 25. Diagram of the POW camp at Sendai #3.

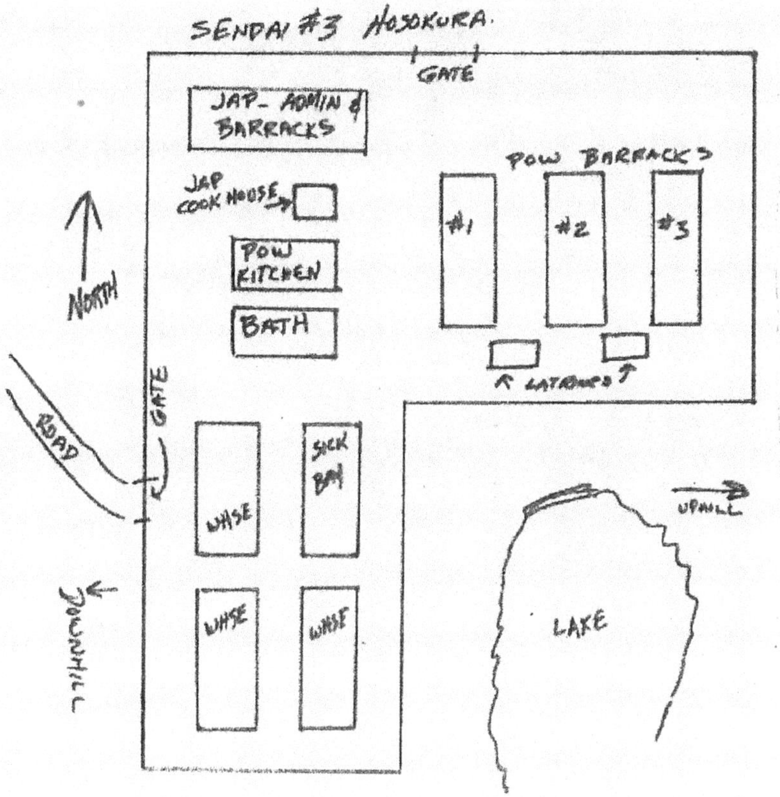

Japanese POW Research Network

Illustration 26. Telegram sent to Burlage's parents with news of their son's liberation from prison camp.

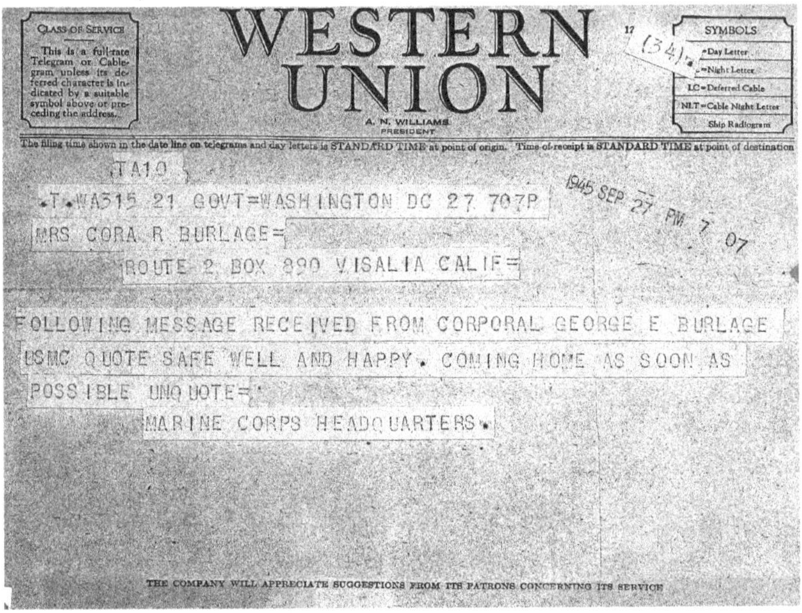

CLASS OF SERVICE

This is a full-rate Telegram or Cablegram unless its deferred character is indicated by a suitable symbol above or preceding the address.

WESTERN UNION

A. N. WILLIAMS PRESIDENT

SYMBOLS
Day Letter
Night Letter
LC=Deferred Cable
NLT=Cable Night Letter
Ship Radiogram

The filing time shown in the date line on telegrams and day letters is STANDARD TIME at point of origin. Time of receipt is STANDARD TIME at point of destination

TA10

.T.WA515 21 GOVT=WASHINGTON DC 27 707P

1945 SEP 27 PM 7 07

MRS CORA R BURLAGE=

ROUTE 2 BOX 890 VISALIA CALIF=

FOLLOWING MESSAGE RECEIVED FROM CORPORAL GEORGE E BURLAGE USMC QUOTE SAFE WELL AND HAPPY. COMING HOME AS SOON AS POSSIBLE UNQUOTE=

MARINE CORPS HEADQUARTERS.

THE COMPANY WILL APPRECIATE SUGGESTIONS FROM ITS PATRONS CONCERNING ITS SERVICE

Burlage Archives

Illustration 27. Telegram sent by George Burlage to his parents after his liberation.

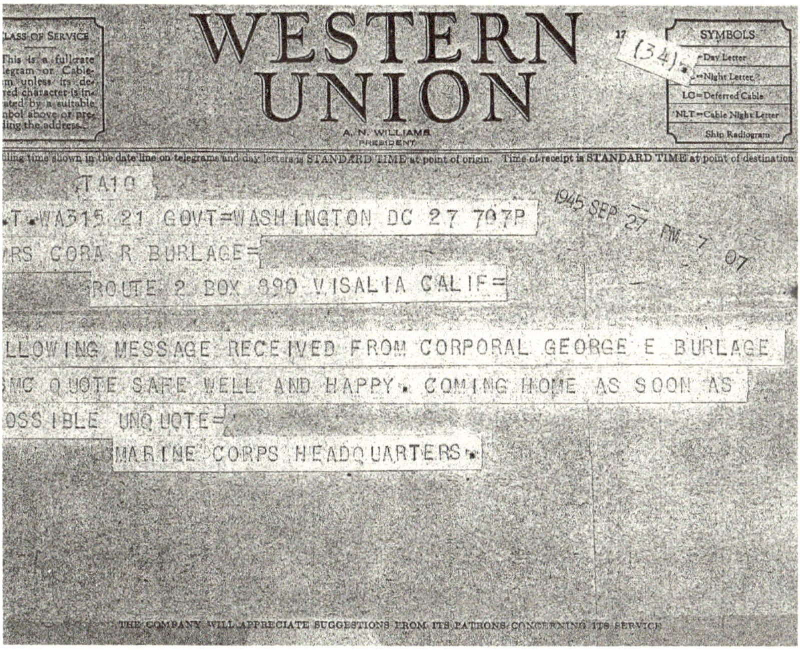

WESTERN UNION

A. N. WILLIAMS, PRESIDENT

SYMBOLS

LC=Deferred Cable

NLT=Cable Night Letter

Ship Radiogram

STANDARD TIME at point of origin. Time of receipt is STANDARD TIME at point of destination

TA10

T WA315 21 GOVT=WASHINGTON DC 27 707P

1945 SEP 27 PM 7 07

RS CORA R BURLAGE=

ROUTE 2 BOX 890 VISALIA CALIF=

LLOWING MESSAGE RECEIVED FROM CORPORAL GEORGE E BURLAGE

MC QUOTE SAFE WELL AND HAPPY. COMING HOME AS SOON AS

OSSIBLE UNQUOTE=

MARINE CORPS HEADQUARTERS.

THE COMPANY WILL APPRECIATE SUGGESTIONS FROM ITS PATRONS CONCERNING ITS SERVICE

Burlage Archives

Illustration 28. *Visalia Times-Delta* article (September 1945) with the news of Burlage's liberation.

George Burlage Is Reported Liberated

In a telegram from Gen. A. A. Vandegrift, commandant of the U. S. Marine Corps, Mr. and Mrs. George S. Burlage of route 2, box 266-A were informed today that their son, Cpl. George Edward Burlage, USMC, has been liberated from a prison camp in Japan and arrived in Guam on September 16, en route to the United States.

Corporal Burlage, a graduate of the local high school and junior college, enlisted in the Marine Corps on August 18, 1939, and was sent overseas the next December 4. He was stationed at Cavite on one of the Philippine islands at a navy station. During the last days of the fall of the islands he was taken prisoner by the Japanese and placed in a prison camp at Manila. Last December he was taken to a prison camp in Tokyo.

Since being a prisoner of war, Burlage has been able to send only a few cards to his parents. The last of those short messages from him was received last January.

A brother, Warrant Officer Robert E. Burlage, is now in the Philippine islands, having been overseas the last time since August. He was on a navy transport, but is now on a floating drydock. He entered the navy service 12 years ago and took part in four invasions in the war.

Burlage Archives

Illustration 29. George Burlage's official prisoner-of-war record.

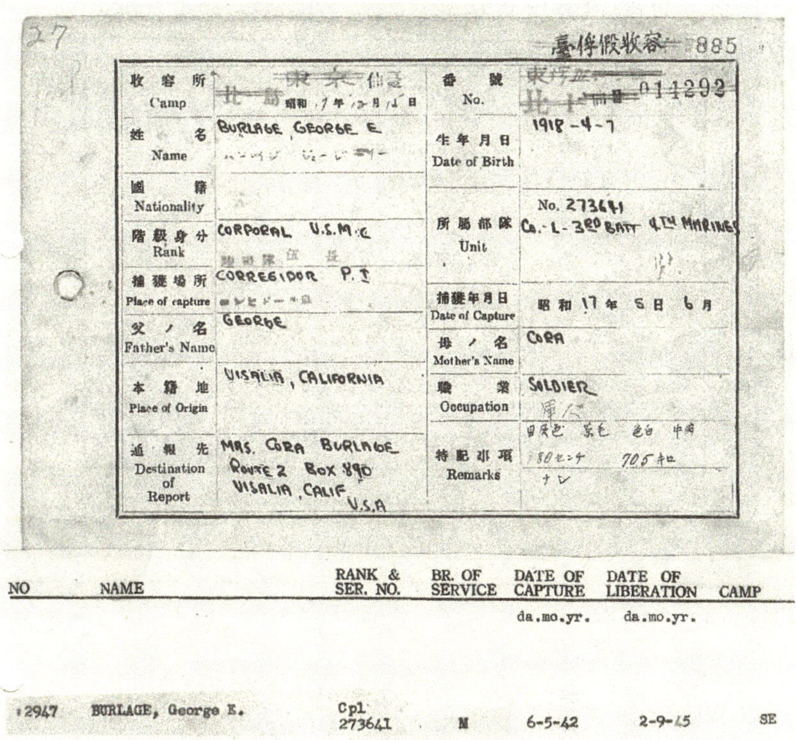

885

收容所 Camp	昭和 17年 12月 15日	番號 No.	011292
姓名 Name	BURLAGE, GEORGE E.	生年月日 Date of Birth	1918-4-7
國籍 Nationality			
階級身分 Rank	CORPORAL U.S.M.C.	所屬部隊 Unit	No. 273641 Co. L - 3RD BATT 4TH MARINES
捕獲場所 Place of capture	CORREGIDOR P.I.	捕獲年月日 Date of Capture	昭和 17年 5日 6月
父ノ名 Father's Name	GEORGE	母ノ名 Mother's Name	CORA
本籍地 Place of Origin	VISALIA, CALIFORNIA	職業 Occupation	SOLDIER 軍人
通報先 Destination of Report	MRS. CORA BURLAGE ROUTE 2 BOX 890 VISALIA, CALIF. U.S.A	特記事項 Remarks	180センチ 70.5キロ

NO	NAME	RANK & SER. NO.	BR. OF SERVICE	DATE OF CAPTURE	DATE OF LIBERATION	CAMP
				da.mo.yr.	da.mo.yr.	
2947	BURLAGE, George E.	Cpl 273641	M	6-5-42	2-9-45	SE

Georgianne Burlage
The document was given to his daughter by representatives of Japan's Ministry of Health, Labour, and Welfare in September 2019.

Illustration 30. Burlage's official history of POW camp transfers as recorded on the back of his POW record.

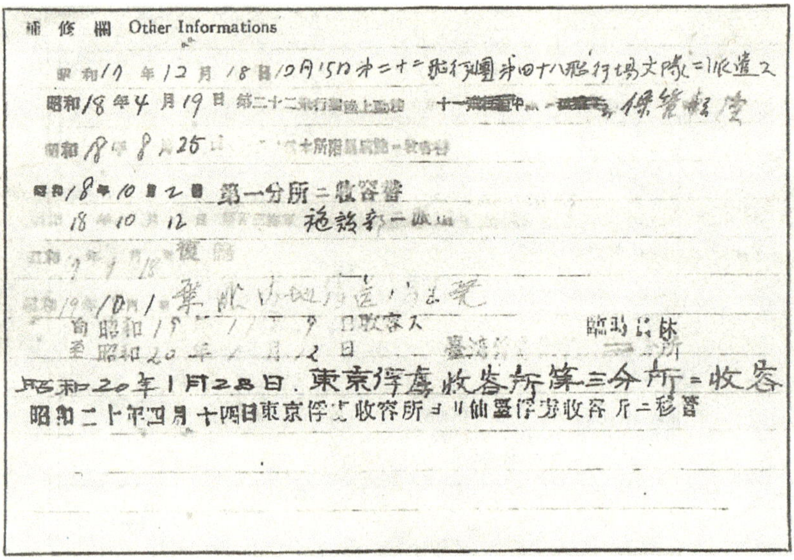
補修欄 Other Informations

[illegible]

昭和18年10月2日 第一分所ニ収容替

[illegible]

昭和20年1月28日 東京俘虜収容所第三分所ニ収容

昭和二十年四月十四日東京俘虜収容所ヨリ仙台俘虜収容所ニ移管

Georgianne Burlage

Illustration 31. Translation of transfer record.

George Burlage's prisoner-of-war record listing his transfers

(translation)

December 18. 1942— transported to Airport #46/big troop

April 19, 1943-- worked at Airport #22

August 25, 1943-- transported to Manila (Bilibid)

October 2, 1943-- transported to the first branch camp (Cabanatuan)

October 12, 1943-- transported to #103 navy facility (Las Pinas)

September 18, 1944-- returned to original camp

October 1, 1944-- taken to ship for transport to Japan

From November 9. 1944, to January 12, 1945—

contained in the camp at Sendai POW temporary camp

January 28, 1945— contained in Tokyo POW third branch camp

April 14, 1945— officially transferred to Sendai POW status from Tokyo POW status

Georgianne Burlage. Translation by Ayako Kobayashi

Illustration 32. *Visalia Times-Delta* article on the reunion of George and Robert Burlage.

Brothers Together After 8½ Years

A happy family reunion was held at the George S. Burlage home, Route 2, Visalia, over the last weekend when the two sons of Mr. and Mrs. Burlage visited them. It was the first time the two young men had been together in 8½ years.

Carpenter Warrant Officer Robert E. Burlage, U. S. Navy, and Platoon Sergeant George E. Burlage, U. S. Marine Corps, have a total of 20 years in the services, Robert 13 and George seven. Of this, the two have 17 years outside the United States, and also wear 18 campaign and service ribbons.

It was the first time the two had met since New Year's Day in 1938. That meeting was shortly after Robert had returned home after 32 months of duty with the Asiatic fleet. Later he was sent to the east coast for duty and eventually to the neutrality patrol in the Atlantic. George enlisted in the marines and was sent to the Philippine islands.

After the war started both were in action, George with the Fourth Marine regiment in the Philippines, and Robert on the naval transport USS Mount Vernon on which he helped take English reinforcements to Singapore, leaving there only six days before the fortress surrendered. He circled the globe to get back to San Francisco. During the remainder of the war he was with amphibious groups in the Pacific theater. Since the end of the war he has been in the Philippines, returning to the U. S. a few weeks ago.

George, who has been back since October last year, when he was liberated from the Japanese who took him and his outfit prisoners, met Robert in San Francisco last Tuesday.

Robert left Sunday for San Diego where he will return to duty status with his prewar rating of chief shipfitter, and George returned to San Francisco to resume duties with the Marine Corps headquarters department of the Pacific.

Mrs. Robert E. Burlage accompanied the two fighting men home. The brothers also visited their sisters, Mrs. Ruth Diaz and Mrs. Lois Brase.

Both brothers retired from the military after twenty years of service.

Illustration 33. Burlage's return to Corregidor in 1952 as a Marine Corps staff writer.

Burlage Archives
Burlage is in the back row wearing a camera strap.

Illustration 34. Msgt. George Burlage's USMC reenlistment photo in 1959.

Burlage Archives

Illustration 35. Photo of Las Pinas camp location.

Burlage Archives

The camp was located by Nichols Field near Manila near what is now the Ninoy Aquino International Airport.

Illustration 36. Malinta Tunnel in 1967.

Burlage Archives

Illustration 37. Ruins of the Mile-Long Barracks on Corregidor in 2017.

Georgianne Burlage

Illustration 38. Location of the 92nd Garage on Corregidor.

Georgianne Burlage

The 92nd Garage is where the Japanese held the prisoners for days before taking them to POW camps.

Illustration 39. Battery Crockett on Corregidor where Burlage was assigned in 1942.

Georgianne Burlage

Illustration 40. Mount Samat—the site of a national memorial to the American and Filipino troops who fought on the Bataan Peninsula.

Georgianne Burlage
Bataan was surrendered on April 9, 1942.

Illustration 41. The piers behind the Manila Hotel.

Georgianne Burlage
Many of the hell ships (including Burlage's) departed from these piers.

Illustration 42. Georgianne Burlage by the commemorative plaque honoring the prisoners held at Sendai #3.

Georgianne Burlage

Illustration 43. The path taken by Sendai #3 prisoners to report for work at the Hosokura mine.

Georgianne Burlage

Illustration 44. Entrance to Hosokura mine.

Georgianne Burlage
Burlage was beaten in front of the entrance for insulting Tojo.

Illustration 45. Photo of Bataan taken on a Corregidor beach.

Georgianne Burlage

Illustration 46. George Burlage at his USMC retirement in 1959.

Burlage Archive
He served twenty years in the Corps.

Chapter Nine

No Thanks, Cabanatuan

"How is it to live behind barbed wire? I saw death, lived it, lived with it, tasted it for forty months."

George Burlage

The new prisoners-of-war quickly fell into two categories—the ones who had already given up and the ones who were determined to survive.

Cabanatuan and Camp O'Donnell were two especially inhumane prisoner-of-war camps. O'Donnell was the destination of the Bataan Death March and had a high death rate. Cabanatuan was also brutal and as with O'Donnell, disease and starvation were common. The death rate for the Corregidor prisoners was lower than for those on the Bataan Death March because they were captured a month after Bataan fell. However, the Corregidor prisoners' mortality rate soon began to rise.

George Burlage arrived at Cabanatuan in late May 1942 and quickly realized that he had to be transferred to another camp if he wanted to survive. A new camp was being established on the

island of Palawan. He reasoned that no place could be worse than Cabanatuan, and soon he was asking to be transferred.

My forty months of slave labor began at Cabanatuan. I saw death, smelled it, lived with it for forty months.

From the first day of my captive life, I had the confidence that I would make it. I could anticipate, plan, and accept the challenge. You had to have faith in yourself. You had to live it one day at a time knowing that today and tomorrow will be a repeat of yesterday but one day closer to freedom. Death, we knew, could strike at any time. Luck played a part, too. How can I explain my survival when so many died? Fate?

I entered Cabanatuan mid-afternoon on May 27, 1942. I was feeling the effects of vitamin deficiency especially with my vision. Adequate food was a distant memory. I guessed that I had lost fifty pounds during the siege of Corregidor, and I really needed a shower. Being yelled at in a language that I did not understand and then beaten because I didn't follow directions was becoming tiresome. This was Cabanatuan Camp #3 (there were three sections), and it was formerly a training camp for the Philippine Army. The buildings were constructed of bamboo and nipa, and bamboo mats served for a floor and sleeping space and would soon be home to millions of bedbugs. There was a shortage of water (one spigot for every 1,500 men) and a ration of 1000 calories per day. The camp had a daily death rate of thirty to forty prisoners. There was little sanitation, and mud and blow flies soon appeared.

Everyone was downhearted, and death seemed to be the easy way out. To cheer up the prisoners, rumors began. We were told that Russia was now in the war, that the U.S. Fourth Army had landed in Batangas and was fighting towards Manila. The one that most people believed was that arrangements were being made to send the prisoners to Ecuador, a neutral nation, for return to the U.S. The rumors were fantastic, but they did help us.

Cabanatuan was the largest POW camp and at one time housed about 10,000 prisoners. There was a hospital with few facilities, and it was used to segregate the very sick from the rest of the camp population. The routine for the first few weeks consisted mainly of working parties. I volunteered for as many details as I could for several reasons, especially the opportunity to forage for food. The three daily meals were half-cooked rice and a "pipe stem" soup made from sweet potato vines and other vegetation. There was a scarcity of fish and meat, and malnutrition was apparent in the prisoners. The camp was run by Americans under strict Japanese supervision. Bathing was allowed twice weekly in a muddy river at the back of the camp. Saluting and bowing to the guards were required, and if a prisoner failed to show respect, the consequences were harsh. Slapping and being forced to stand in the sun for hours were common disciplines.

The prisoners were assigned to ten-man squads as an escape prevention. The mandate was if one man tried to escape, the other nine were executed. I don't remember anybody attempting to escape. Where would we go? There were three thousand deaths from disease and malnutrition out of a total of ten thousand prisoners at Cabanatuan in 1942. Cabanatuan was unfit for humans. The problem was that far more of us were surrendered than the Japanese had anticipated. Unlike the Shinto Code of Bushido, the Americans, British, and Europeans saw no dishonor in surrender. (By the way, we were surrendered as a fighting force. It wasn't an individual decision.) The buildings were made from bamboo, and the floors had cracks. Japanese and Filipinos rarely had beds in the Western idea of bedding. They slept on mats, so we did, too.

The Japanese for some unknown reason didn't mix the Bataan and Corregidor prisoners. Maybe it was due to the high rate of dysentery among the Bataan survivors. They had been captured a month before us and were in worse physical shape. Keeping records of the prisoners including deaths was left up to the American officers. Few POWs had their dog tags because the Japanese took them when the men were captured, so the identity of the deceased was written on paper and placed in his mouth. The dead were kept in a mortuary to wait for the burial detail to take them to the cemetery. A master list of the deceased prisoners was kept but was incomplete. At first, grave markers were not used, and the bodies were buried in a mass grave It was a daily event. About a year after I left Cabanatuan, the Japanese allowed the prisoners to beautify the cemetery area, and markers, crosses, flowers, and a monument were added. Also, using camp records, many of the older graves were identified. As the war continued, the death rate decreased at Cabanatuan. It also soon became apparent why the Japanese had kept their prisoners alive. Labor details were being formed to work on different projects, mainly airfields, roads, and docks. Groups were also being sent to Manchuria and Japan for mine and factory labor.

I witnessed my gunner and assistant gunner from Corregidor die of dysentery a few days apart. I had to get out of Cabanatuan before I wound up ill or dead. I decided to ask the camp officials for a transfer to another camp and on July 31, 1942, I was aboard a ship heading to the island of Palawan to build an airstrip.

Between 1942 and 1944, 2636 prisoners-of-war are estimated to have died at Cabanatuan. 2399 of these deaths were men captured at Bataan, and 237 were from Corregidor. Within six months after the surrender of Bataan, one-third of the men who surrendered had died.

Chapter Ten

Working for the Emperor at Palawan

"Personally, if I had it to do over, I would have given death a little more consideration. I never would accept that I might not survive. I wasn't going to lose my life behind barbed wire."

George Burlage

At Palawan, the prisoners soon realized that they were on the island for slave labor. The island was 350 miles from Cabanatuan and extremely isolated, and an airfield was needed for the Japanese war effort. Against the rules of the Geneva Accords stating that POWs could not be used as laborers or as part of their captors' war effort, the American POWs were to build the airfield.

After being given an axe, a pick, and a sun hat, George Burlage was ordered to start working. The prisoners worked sunrise to sunset seven days a week on near-starvation rations. The work was slow and difficult, and the prisoners made sure that the airfield would not be completed quickly.

Several prisoners were beaten and tortured for stealing food from the camp provisions or taking fresh fruit from the island's trees. A few prisoners were executed for trying to escape, but the prisoners soon realized that there was nowhere to go. They were Guests of the Emperor, and the Emperor needed the POWs' labor to assist in the war efforts.

I had quickly realized that I had to get out of Cabanatuan if I had any hopes of survival. I left Cabanatuan in July with 200 other prisoners for Puerto Princesa on the southern Philippine island of Palawan. The trip took five days aboard the *Sanko Maru*, a converted troop transport, and we stopped to unload supplies at a leper colony. The task for these POWs was to build an airfield for the Japanese Army. We were told that this would be a three-month-detail and considering the circumstances, the experience would be enjoyable. This wasn't at all how things turned out.

Puerto Princesa was the provincial capital of the island of Palawan. Magellan's ships allegedly landed there in 1521 to search for provisions. Ten thousand residents had lived in Puerto Princesa before the war and were Catholic although the island itself was predominantly Islamic. The place was soon deserted as the Japanese approached in early 1942, the residents fleeing to nearby hills.

We were quartered in the now deserted Philippine Constabulary while the Japanese soldiers took over the high school building across the plaza. The barracks were in poor condition, but the deck was sound. We helped with repairs to the piping and water and also constructed a galley and toilet and bathing facilities. The routine for the first few days was the series of formations that the Japanese military always forced the prisoners to learn. We were also informed about the usual warnings of punishment. Too soon, we started to work in the jungle. The POWs were issued wheelbarrows, shovels, and grubbing hoes as equipment to build an airfield in the thick jungle. On August 8, 1942, we started to work on the promised three-month construction project that eventually lasted two-and-a-half years. The Japanese wouldn't confirm that we were building an airfield, but we figured it out. American prisoners-of-war were slave laborers for the Japanese war effort which was illegal according to the Geneva Accords.

An average workday began before daylight. I would get up, go outside to the latrine, and tried to clean myself with limited soap and water. By the time I returned to the barracks, a bucket or two with watery soup and rice was waiting. That was our breakfast. After our meal, the trucks would drive up, and off we went four or five miles away from the camp, out in the boondocks, and started to work. Every day was the same—cutting down coconut trees with a grubbing hoe, shoveling and pushing dirt in a wheelbarrow, and leveling off the ground for the airfield. Midmorning, there was a fifteen- minute break when tea was offered to us. Then it was back to work for a few hours, then buckets of rice arrived for our noon meal. Around sundown, we gathered up our tools and walked back to our barracks. There were showers by the barracks, and we all utilized them because we were covered with dirt every day. We then had dinner and discussed what food we were going to eat when we got home. I never became used to being hungry. Every day was the same—monotonous. Most of us kept our morale up by thinking of when we would be back in the United States.

We had been promised good—at least edible—food. The food wasn't awful at the start of our stay, but there was never enough. Our interpreter told us that all our concerns and suggestions would be submitted to the camp commander, but nothing changed. In August 1942, the Japanese government changed our "captive" status to that of "prisoner-of-war." Nothing changed then, either.

Soon after our arrival in Palawan's deserted capital, a few POWs escaped, only to be recaptured and executed. I couldn't understand how these men thought they could hide among the Filipinos. For example, I had reddish blonde hair and blue eyes. I certainly couldn't blend in. The prisoners were lined up, and the camp commandant told the man that he was insulted by their actions. He offered three courses of action:

1. He would forget what happened, and the men could go back to work.
2. He could put the men in chains to work.
3. He could force the prisoners to stay in the barracks and starve.

He warned us that he was capable of any of these plus setting our barracks on fire and killing us all. The commandant shouted, "Remember what our forces did to you at Pearl Harbor!"

We finally went back to work after three days of starvation.

Everywhere, thick vegetation of undergrowth grew. Bananas, papaya trees, and coconut trees grew in abundance, and ants, bugs, monkeys, and snakes were numerous. It was the POWs' job to clear and level the ground and then build a concrete runway with picks, axes, hoes, and wheelbarrows. The day for the groundbreaking arrived with a special ceremony. All American prisoners and Japanese soldiers were required to attend the ceremony. A senior American officer had warned us that we might find the ceremony to be amusing but to be sure not to laugh.

As the prisoners stood at attention, the Japanese soldiers fell in formation and presented alms to the spirits. A Japanese doctor then took the leading role, prayed, and cast raw rice into the wind. Then taking a hoe, the doctor chopped a few weeds and after another presentation of alms, the ceremony was over. The "spirit" would protect the workers, and no misfortune would happen. No one laughed, but there was unconcealed amusement on our faces. The prisoners were equipped with hoes to clean the jungle to prepare for the construction of two runways. Each runway was to be 1200 meters long and 70 meters wide. In addition to clearing land for runways, more land had to be prepared for buildings and approaches. I wondered if the Japanese believed that this airfield would be built before the Americans returned.

The Japanese commandant announced that the abundant fruit in the jungle was off-limits to the prisoners. Rice and weed soup were the only food that the POWs were allowed to consume, and fruit-eaters would be shot. The men argued that the fruit was needed to prevent beriberi, pellagra, and other nutrition-deficient diseases, but the Japanese position did not change. We soon proved that a hungry American is crafty and became experts at theft while being supervised. However, some were caught.

A three-star private, Nishitani, was in charge of the Japanese and American galleys (kitchens). When a cook caught two Americans stealing a papaya from a tree in our camp, Nishitani decided to punish the men by breaking their left arms with an iron bar and then beating them. The men were sent to Manila for additional punishment. Another prisoner was beaten because he would not admit that the United States was losing the war.

As the jungle got deeper and hotter, the days got longer. The men were restless, but little serious thought was given to escaping, especially after the Japanese warnings. However, six men did escape. The guards attempted to find the prisoners, but their fear of the jungle prevented a thorough search. The remaining prisoners were punished by reduced rations. Two more escaped, and mass starvations were imposed on the POWs. The ten-man groups were initiated. If one of the ten escaped, the other nine were to be killed. That system was successful in stopping escapes. The men assumed that the prisoners who got out joined with the Filipino resistance in the hills.

Every day was the same. We were restless and hungry, and we constantly talked about good meals, cold beer, our futures, and home. The Japanese continued their strict and harsh rules and starvation rations. It was a hard, monotonous existence. I even killed some of my fellow prisoners, but not in the way you might think. We were given daily food rations (usually rice balls) and cigarette rations. Never having been a smoker, I traded my cigarettes for more food. I'm not sure if the reduction of food really caused any smokers' premature deaths, but some men did choose nicotine over nourishment.

The prisoners were starving, and most thought of little else than finding food. Some POWs discovered a way into the Japanese storeroom and stole canned meat. They were soon caught and imprisoned in the compound brig to await punishment. The next Saturday, we were given the day off. It was apparent that a show was being planned for us. The men in the brig were brought out and tied to coconut trees in the compound, and several guards under the supervision of a sergeant soon appeared. The sergeant first went to work with a long leather whip on the prisoners. He then sat down and with a drawn pistol pointing at the helplessly tied prisoners, gave orders to his soldiers. They took turns with a pole about eight feet long and 8 ½ inches in diameter.

When a prisoner passed out, water was poured over his head, and the beating would continue. After the public beatings, the prisoners were returned to their cells. However, a Japanese officer visited the cells, forced the men on their feet, and then knocked them down. In a few days, the men were sent to Fort Santiago in Manila for additional punishment. The fort was renowned for sadistic punishment and cruelty. This show was the greatest display of cruelty I witnessed that didn't end in immediate death.

After this incident, life in the compound settled into a rigid routine. An additional hundred prisoners were added to the airfield detail to step up the airfield progress. Also, a detachment of Kempeital (the notorious Japanese military police) and a company of Japanese-sponsored Philippine Constabulary arrived. Escape now seemed impossible.

Even with the additional guards, four more men escaped. Two were recaptured, but the other two stayed at large. The two who were captured, and after very rough treatment by the guards, were sent to Manila for "trial." Not long after this, two more men escaped while at work but were soon caught by the Constabulary. These two were unceremoniously shot. It was very evident that it was plain death to escape. The guerrillas working in the hills just a few miles away also sent word not to escape as it was useless to try. The "bamboo telegraph" did share that the guerrillas had 1,300 trained and armed men waiting for MacArthur's return.

The prisoners began to find other methods not to work and to get transferred from Palawan. Sabotage began. We also knew never to make a work quota because our requirements would just be increased. Our work "week" was ten days on, one day off. I usually attempted to clean up on my day off. Something else needs to be explained. Most of us were still wearing the clothes we had on when captured. I tried to bathe whenever I had a chance, but it was a losing battle. We were filthy and malnourished, the perfect combination for disease.

Chapter Eleven

What We Did to Them

"We knew we couldn't escape, so we had fun tormenting our guards."

George Burlage

The prisoners soon realized that escape was impossible and that every day meant more hard labor. All days were the same and to ease the monotony, the men soon began to think of ideas how to taunt the guards. The pranks were planned to annoy the guards but weren't serious enough for severe punishment.

The seemingly never-ending airstrip construction continued dawn to dusk. Taking fruit off trees was forbidden, and several prisoners received punitive beatings for eating a papaya or mango from one of the hundreds of tropical trees. Food was stolen from storage areas. Even beers disappeared. The POWs were starving.

Palawan was where George Burlage's arm-breaking career began. A broken arm meant that one fewer prisoner could work, slowing down the airfield project and hurting the Japanese war effort. Burlage never broke his own arm, though, at Palawan and in other camps where he was held.

It was obvious that the Japanese thought they could win the war with slave labor. They controlled us physically, but not mentally. The POWs certainly didn't buy into the "we are alive because of the magnanimity of the Emperor" line given us by our guards. The truth was we were alive due to our will and strength and determination to survive.

Sabotage—no riots, no uprisings, just subtle ways to interfere with construction projects or to fool the guards—became common. POWs were used to bolster the Japanese war effort. We were the slave laborers in airfield construction, on shipping docks, and in mines. We reacted quietly.

The most effective and negative effects on the Japanese war efforts were the sick and lame POWs—faked or real—who were unable and unwilling to work as forced laborers. Sickness and sabotage and damage to mine production, tunnel projects, foundries, rails, and shipyards became our targets to deter the Japanese war effort. The results were the dubious rewards of POW labor.

The sabotage efforts at Palawan began while building the airstrip. Vehicles were provided to haul materials, but few Japanese guards had ever driven a car or truck. POWs were assigned to drive the trucks (most of the vehicles were captured American vehicles). To slow down operations, the POW driver would stall out the truck, turned to the ever-present guard, and say, "trucko beoki"—sick truck. He'd tell the guard he could fix it, then get out, raise the hood, and probably clean his fingernails with the screwdriver. Then he would slam the hood, get back in the cab and start the engine with a roar. The guard would be amazed that this stupid American could be so mechanical.

The Palawan camp was isolated and near the equator. An inter-island boat from Manila brought supplies every few months, and the prisoners would become stevedores, unloading machinery, sacks of cement, construction supplies, and food. The prisoners would "accidentally" damage items or tear holes in bags and steal food.

Another method used to avoid work was to pour boiling water on a hand or foot. The result was second-to-third degree burns and was good for a ten-day rest. Another method was to aggravate that Athlete's Foot condition that most prisoners had from working barefoot. Infected or swollen feet slowed men from accomplishing the Japanese construction goals. Athlete's foot was good for a four- or five-day rest. Then there were the "hot water drinking" malaria cases. The "patient" drank hot water to raise his body temperature. Soon, too many prisoners were trying this, and the Japanese guards caught on to the scheme.

Palawan is where I began my "medical career." At one of my future POW camps, I was known as a doctor of "breakology." All this title meant was I became an expert in breaking arms. My "career" began at Palawan. As the Japanese demanded more and more labor, the rations became less and less. Malnutrition was affecting the prisoners both mentally and physically, and the men sought ways to keep from working. The men knew of a fellow prisoner who would break arms if requested. That prisoner was me.

I later described the beginning of my arm-breaking career in a speech:

"Three American prisoners gathered mysteriously in the shadow of the coconut palms. While one man watched for the patrolling Japanese sentries, the other two secretly went about their work. One of the men calmly laid his arm on a log while the other quickly hit the arm with a piece of heavy pipe.

"Coming onto the porch of the lighted barracks, the injured man asked for the American doctor. The doctor diagnosed a severe compound fracture of the left arm. It would be many weeks, possibly never on this rice diet, before this man would be able to work again."

I practiced my arm breaking skills at Palawan and would perfect them at the Los Piñas Camp. It was a satisfactory, almost smug feeling to outwit our guards.

The "no work" list at Palawan continued to grow. Every injury was reported to the Japanese doctors as an "accident" caused by slippery steps, rotten floors, or poor lighting. Men working in the fields while under direct supervision of the Japanese guards also were successful in injuring themselves. Why would a person injure himself? Self-preservation mixed in with a rationalized patriotic feeling of "if I don't work for the enemy, then I won't be helping them fight my country" was the reason. Also, a self-inflicted injury was the only chance we had to rest and to build our strength both physically and mentally. Homemade crutches and improvised splints and slings were crafted. However, an even better method to avoid work was discovered one that caused infection.

The scarcity of vitamins and calories in our diets resulted in easy bruising, and these bruises often lead to infections. Adding battery acid to these infected bruises resulted in large, ugly, infectious skin ulcers. Swelling was common, resulting in a recovery period of several weeks.

One of our best "what we did to them" moments was Thanksgiving Day, 1942. I later shared the story in an article I wrote for *Leatherneck* magazine 10 years later.

A POW Thanksgiving Story

Americans, whatever their circumstances, have a way of observing Thanksgiving Day. For American prisoners of war confined in a World War II Japanese labor camp, their way of toasting the Pilgrim Fathers had explosive results that reached into the heart of Imperial Army headquarters.

It all began on Thanksgiving Day, 1942, in a work camp on the isolated island of Palawan in the Southern Philippines. The day was spent in routine dawn-to-dusk labor, much like those which preceded it and the many more that would follow.

The jungle airstrip that the 250 or so American prisoners, mostly survivors of the Fourth Marines captured at Corregidor by the Japanese Imperial Army, were building was thousands of miles from Mom and her home cooking. That day the great distance and near-hopeless situation only served to emphasize the talk of sitting down to the family table once more.

After a never-satisfying supper of rice and "weed" soup, the prisoners gathered in group and in the faint light of the naked bulbs that grew dimmer with each beat of the wheezing generator. While the devout gathered to give spiritual thanks, others talked of home and family feasts. Later, as each man crawled into his allotted space— a 30" x 80" area on the bare floor— to sleep, he dreamed of better times, both past and future. No one dreamed of tomorrow and of a belated Thanksgiving treat that would shake the Philippine headquarters of the Imperial Army.

With the first rays of the equatorial sun, the prisoner of war camp burst into routine activity as tired Americans readied themselves for another day. The usual breakfast of rice was rationed out to the man, followed by a quick trek to the jungle clearing and work.

Midway through the morning toil, an excited interpreter called all men to quit their work and return to camp. An inter-island steamer, confiscated from its Filipino owner at the start of the war, had just cleared the entrance to Puerta Princesa Bay and was heading for the isolated camp's dock with the first supplies since early summer.

Quickly assembled on the dock, the prisoners were counted into working parties to work in the ship's holds, as topside stevedores, winch operators and net men. The remaining men were detailed to the barracks area to unload and store the goods as they were brought there by truck.

Satisfied with the arrangements, the Japanese soldiers returned to the shade of coconut palms growing at the foot of the docks. From this shady, but strategic, spot they could control the activities of their sweating captives while escaping the heat, made more unbearable by the reflecting lights of the bay.

Little did the guards realize that their action would keep them "dry" several months—until the next ship supply arrived—and start a string of red tape flowing that would be the envy of any American bureaucrat.

From the ships' holds the prisoners brought thousands of bags of cement, enough to start the initial sidings for the proposed airstrip. In another hold were sacks of rice and some special Oriental delicacies especially ordered by the prison camp commandant.

Included in the supply were enough delicacies for a party for the Japanese soldiers. As the drooling prisoners carefully unloaded the party trimmings, their thoughts returned to Thanksgiving Day... and then suddenly they spied a gold mine! Neatly stacked in the corner of the hold were several cases of San Miguel, one of the Philippine's best-known products. The tired, sweating prisoners didn't hesitate to exploit their find. Why not quench a long-standing thirst and at the same time drink a belated toast to the Pilgrim Fathers and Thanksgiving Day?

By rotating the unloading crews from the hold at frequent intervals, all prisoners managed to get a brief pause at the "corner bar." The guards, still lounging in the cool shade, never noticed any lag in unloading and the nipping and toasting continued uninterrupted.

As each bottle was emptied, the cap was replaced, and the bottle returned to the reusable cardboard case. Finally, as the work of unloading neared completion, the cases of empty bottles were loaded onto a truck. When the soldiers saw the cases as the truck moved off the dock, they shouted at the prisoners, jeering them by informing them that only the conquerors were entitled to a man's drink.

This stage for their party was set that night in the neighboring Japanese barracks. Buckets of steamed rice, plus tidbits of salted plums and dried fish, were brought to start the first round of festivities. The beer, followed by dancing with each other at the womanless outpost, would come later. Merriment, mingled with childish glee, was short-lived that night. There was no beer to fan the flames of the planned revelry and disappointed soldiers, like every other night for several months, turned in early.

The only official explanation of the empty beer cases was that they were put on the ship by mistake when it left Manila. A full report of the discrepancy was made, necessitating the exchange of reams of reports between Imperial Army headquarters in Manila and the isolated prisoner of war labor camp. Each report, prepared in Japanese language characters, was laboriously written by harassed office clerks. Never once was the integrity of the captive Americans—those who had remembered to toast their Pilgrim Fathers—ever questioned. Another American custom had survived.

That beer, although a bit warm, surely was better than that locomotive gin that we were stilling and drinking. It gave us a buzz but not much more.

I was at Palawan with my old friend Sgt. John Hughes from Cavite who I regarded as my mentor. We talked every morning before heading out to work. Hughes had a morning ritual. He would take out his pocket Bible (what was left of it), tear out a page, read the front and back, tear the page in half, and roll two papaya leaf cigarettes.

Hughes always told me the same advice every morning. He warned, "George, get out of here if you can. They are going to kill us when the Americans return." The sergeant believed that the isolation and remote location would be the prisoners' death sentence. He viewed Palawan as a potential death camp. His prophecies were proven true in December 1944 when the Japanese massacred 139 prisoners-of-war at the Palawan camp. Hughes did not survive although eleven POWs escaped.

In late August 1943, I developed dengue fever. Dengue fever is virtually unknown in the United States, usually brought in by tourists. However, the disease is common in the tropics and spread through infected mosquitoes. My condition was so severe that the Japanese transferred me to the Bilibid prison hospital in Manila. I traveled on an inter-island ferry with thirty fellow prisoners. Some of the men who left the island did so reluctantly, believing that Palawan would be one of the Philippine locations to be liberated first when the Americans returned. I felt fortunate that I had been able to depart, but I was sad to leave my friends.

Chapter Twelve

Back to Bilibid

"Can the story of the prisoner-of-war really be told? There were close to 130,000 of us in World War II who spent days to several years with their captors, each with many similarities but yet individual effects. We met the enemy face-to-face and had physical contact with this enemy. I was wearing khaki trousers, shirt, and shoes without socks when we were surrendered—no hat or helmet —but damned well dressed to how I would be later on."

George Burlage

After a year on Palawan, George Burlage began to become anxious. The island was very isolated and had very little outside communication.

George had developed beriberi, malaria, and pellagra, diseases caused by vitamin deficiencies and mosquitoes. He used his illnesses as a ticket to leave Palawan. In the summer of 1942, he was sent to Bilibid in Manila for treatment.

He left many friends behind on Palawan. Most of them were killed in the Palawan Massacre in December 1944.

George Burlage spent several months at Bilibid receiving treatment by the captured doctors and nurses who were the medical staff at the prison. Medicine was scarce, but he did recover through the skilled care of the staff. His health was restored as was his strength. While in Manila, George worked as a landscaper at the Japanese headquarters, creating a rising sun out of flowers and plants.

His next camp was to one that was known as being cruel and brutal, Las Pinas outside of Manila. More airfield construction was in his future, and George perfected his arm-breaking skills.

Manila had changed in the almost two years since I had last been there. The skyline looked familiar, but the city was quiet. The once familiar route from the port area to the main part of Manila through 12th St. and Quezon Boulevard was deserted. There were no rushing, American-built taxicabs which were so numerous in pre-war Manila. Instead, the taxis were man-powered bicycles, pedicabs, or rickshaws. The streets were nearly empty except for uniformed Japanese or Filipinos wearing the designated armband issued to "the right people."

The sick prisoners were taken to Bilibid prison because Bilibid had the most efficient and best trained medical staff of any prison camp with the complete pre-war staff at the Cavite U.S. Naval Hospital. Most of the staff had been POWs since the fall of Manila when they were captured at Santa Scholastica College which had served as their improvised hospital. These doctors and nurses attained the respect and praise of all the prisoners who passed through Bilibid. With little medicine but conscious of their oath and with their knowledge, they saved many lives.

Bilibid Prison had been built in the 1860s during the Spanish colonial era. It featured a twenty-foot guard tower, and the cement cells extended from this tower like spokes on a wheel. Each cell could hold more than ten men, and men slept on the concrete floors unless a makeshift bed could be constructed. As many as 13,000 prisoners-of-war were processed at Bilibid and sent to other camps.

I was in Bilibid for several months and did recover. The medical staff had few methods to treat malaria and vitamin deficiencies. The most common treatments were rest, quinine (the supply of quinine was dwindling), and skilled nursing. Also, the staff attempted to provide nutritional food, but that was scarce, too. While in Manila, a few other POWs and I re-landscaped the lawn of the Japanese Commanding General in the Philippines headquarters at the gutted Far East University buildings. We dug up the lawn outside the offices and replanted it in a rising sun pattern.

The Bilibid doctors attempted to get the stronger and recovered patients out of the prison hospital as quickly as possible. The rice ration there was 450 grams daily (15 ounces), and there was a shortage of food. Those prisoners who were healthier were sent to Cabanatuan so after a month at Bilibid, I was sent back to Cabanatuan. I had weighed 200 pounds and was 6 feet, two when I enlisted in the USMC in 1939. My estimated weight in 1943 was 130 pounds. I was considered "healthier."

Cabanatuan had changed since May 1942. Camp #3 had been closed due to nearby guerrilla activity. All prisoners—Bataan and Corregidor survivors—were in one camp. The only new arrivals were men from work details or those too sick to work. The men at the camp grew vegetables for sale (the camp got a percentage.) At the back of the camp was a cemetery containing more than 2,800 Americans who had died at Cabanatuan. Once again, I knew that I had to get out of that camp if I were to survive.

My parents George S. and Rebecca Burlage had received official notice in May 1942 that I was missing-in-action. For more than a year, they had no updates on my status. In June 1943, the American Red Cross relayed the news to my parents that I was a prisoner-of-war of the Japanese and were also provided with an address where they could write to me. I guess any letters sent to me were lost in the mail.

Ironically, my parents received a letter in July 1943 that I had mailed a month before the Pearl Harbor attack. I wrote in the note that I was still at Cavite and expected to return to the United States on the next transport.

In late July 1943, another letter arrived in Visalia. The Times-Delta shared the news, and my mother saved the article:

A postcard, with the type writing on it barely legible, received from Corporal George E. Burlage, USMC by his sister Mrs. Lois Brase, brings the first news the Burlage family has had from the Marine who is interned in the Philippines.

Corporal Burlage was reported missing in action since May 1942 until a few weeks ago when his parents, Mr. and Mrs. George S. Burlage of the Ivanhoe district, were notified by the War Department that he was a prisoner of the Japanese.

The card, an Imperial Japanese Army card for prisoners with a printed form to be filled by typewriter, read:

"I am interned at the Philippine Military Prison No 10A.

"My health is good.

"I am uninjured.

"I am well.

"Please see that my private and personal belongings are taking care of.

"Trust everyone is okay. Are you continuing your education?

"Please give my best regards to friends and ex-school instructors."

The card was addressed to his sister, Lois, who was married in May to Mr. David Brase. The two reside near her parents' home.

Corporal Burlage was born April 7, 1918, near Visalia. He is a graduate of Visalia high school and Visalia Junior College. He enlisted in the US Marine Corps on August 18, 1939 and was sent to the Philippine Islands on December 4, 1939. He was stationed at the Cavite Naval Base before the attack on Pearl Harbor.

Three letters and a cable were received from him, after the war began, the last being written February 4, 1942. He has two sisters living near Visalia—

Mrs. Ruth Dias and Mrs. Lois Brase. His brother, Chief Petty Officer Robert Burlage, is somewhere in the Pacific with the U.S. Navy.

The prison camp mentioned was Puerta Princesa on Palawan. This would be my last communication home for almost a year.

My parents received this letter:

25 June 1943

My dear Mr. Burlage:

A partial list of American prisoners of war in the Manila Bay area has just been received from the international Red Cross, containing the name of your son, Corporal George E. Burlage, U.S. Marine Corps, confirming the fact that he is a prisoner-of-war.

The report fails to state the place of internment, but you may communicate with him by mail at the following address:

Corporal George E. Burlage, U.S. Marine Corps,

Interned in the Philippine Islands

C/O the Japanese Red Cross

Tokyo, Japan

via New York, New York

When further information is received regarding your son's welfare, the Prisoners of War Information Bureau, Office of the Provost Marshall General, War Department, Washington, DC, will communicate with you.

Sincerely yours,

C.P. Lancaster,

Captain, U.S. Marine Corps

Needless to add—we never received any mail. The few occasions when Red Cross care packages arrived, our guards enjoyed tormenting us by opening the packages in our presence, checking what had been sent, then keeping the contents.

Chapter Thirteen

The Worst Camp

"I had survived while most did not. No blueprints or rules existed for survival. There was no road map to get you from sunrise to sunset. What you did today to survive could get you killed tomorrow."

George Burlage

Las Pinas lived up to its brutal reputation. The conditions were inhospitable, the food was scarce and inedible, and the work was backbreaking. The prisoners were ordered to drain rice paddies and build an airfield. The tools were primitive, and morale was low.

Filipino POWs worked with Americans, and both had the same goal—not to accomplish much. Survey posts were knocked over or incorrectly placed, concrete was mixed without following directions, and sabotage was common. The men had been prisoners for more than two years and were hoping that the American military would return to the Philippines soon.

George Burlage became the camp's arm breaker but never broke his own. By the time the Japanese had figured out that the arms

were being intentionally broken, the American invasion of the Philippines had begun, and the POWs were facing an unimaginable fate.

George wanted out of Las Pinas. It was by far the worst camp that he was in. When they saw the beautiful American bombers flying over us in the fall of 1944, the POWs were sure that their liberation would be soon. However, the Japanese had other plans for the prisoners, something that they could have never foreseen.

After three days, I joined the two hundred Cabanatuan prisoners who were transferred to join the 600 POWs on another airfield project. The Japanese Navy officials had trucks waiting for us at the Manila station and without even time to stretch, we were hustled into trucks and driven to the south of Manila.

I was uneasy as we approached Nichols Field. We knew that the Japanese Navy had a work camp there with some of the hardest-driving, cruelest guards possible. We were headed to the barrio of Las Piñas where the Japanese Navy was constructing an auxiliary airfield next to Nichols.

The Japanese Navy guards were the meanest. They were famous for their "water treatment" which consisted of sticking a water hose in the victim's mouth and filling him with water. As the man lay in agony, the guard would jump on his stomach, causing the water to squirt out. It was usually fatal, but was a long, lingering death process. Also, the guards were known to be fond of beatings and of the "sun-treatment." This "treatment" included tying the victim's thumbs to a post and allowing the flies and brutal sun to torture the person. This was the sort of camp that we were now going to.

The prisoners were ordered out of the trucks when they arrived at Las Piñas and were told to walk to the barracks. Most of the men had no shoes, and the mud was deep and the gravel rough. I cursed out loud at the guards and yelled that I'd been in cleaner pig pens at home.

The barracks were built in four rows with four rooms each. Fifty men were to occupy each room, sleeping in three rows, side-by-side, feet touching heads. Water was scarce. The rations were set at 600 grams of rice and 120 grams of vegetables daily, but the prisoners never received that much.

The actual airfield project covered an area of two miles in both directions in the middle of rice fields. The first step was to break down the ridges that held water in the paddies. This meant wading in water above the knees all day even in a tropical rainstorm or a blowing typhoon. After a rain, the men trampled through the mud for four to five kilometers. At night the sun hardened the ground into sharp formations. With sore and painful feet, the men would limp back to camp with a sadistic Japanese guard beating on the stragglers with his "vitamin stick" (a club).

Soon, 2,000 Formosans and a few hundred Filipinos were added to the 800 POWs. The Americans and Formosans did the manual labor while the Filipinos were surveyors and carpenters. It soon became obvious that the Filipinos were doing more sabotage than actual work. Their measurements were off, and the carpenters only worked if being watched. Even while being watched by a guard, a Filipino might go through the motions of sawing lumber by using the back of his saw instead of the cutting edge. The Filipinos kept up our morale by their attitude towards the Japanese and their optimism that the Americans would soon invade. Also, the "bamboo telegraph" was providing news of Allied victories in the Pacific and at Normandy. The messages usually concluded with, "It won't be long now. MacArthur is coming." Mac needed to speed things up, I thought.

Building an airfield in the middle of a rice field was difficult. The paddies had to be drained then the land leveled. Worn-out wheelbarrows, homemade shovels, and baskets were used. Eventually, the Japanese brought in small tracked mining cars to assist in moving dirt. Japanese surveyors checked the level of the airfield as the work continued. Their survey stakes placed along the proposed path of the runway were knocked out of line by prisoners or were driven deeper into the ground on purpose. This changed the level of the runway, resulting in one half of the airfield being higher than the other half. When we got close to a survey stake, we gave it a tap to knock it out of line or a sharp tap to change its depth. Part of the runway was never finished. The Filipinos section was two to three inches higher than ours—on purpose.

The Las Piñas camp commandant, a pre-war official in the Bank of Japan in Manila, promised the prisoners upon arrival that they would be paid and would be able to buy tobacco and local edible items on a monthly basis. My first buy was a bag of peanuts, which cost me 20 centavos a canteen cup. Coconuts were 25 centavos, and tobacco was one peso per package. Soon, the prices inflated by 100 to 200 percent.

Too much money and too much demand put the commissary out of business. The prisoners were paid ten to fifteen centavos a day, but the influx of money would come from other sources. For example, a POW working in the motor pool would borrow money from anyone who would sign a note. A Filipino working with him would exchange the note with a counterfeiter in Manila resulting in the POW having thousands of pesos hidden in his G string.

I revived my arm breaking career at Las Pinas, and I suppose that I became legendary. In the late 1990s, an official from the History Division of the Fourth Marines attended— uninvited— a national Fourth Marines reunion in San Antonio. The official walked over to me and said, "Now we know who did it." He was referring to the mystery of a series of broken arms at the Las Piñas camp. For years, the Fourth Marines' historians had tried to discover the identity of the arm breaker. I had kept the secret, but one of my fellow POWs finally divulged the secret after more than fifty years.

In 1998, I was attending the dedication of the National Prisoner-of-War Museum at Andersonville, Georgia, when a reporter from the Dallas ABC affiliate called our house wanting to interview me about my role as a saboteur in POW camps. My daughter shared the message with me the next time I checked in at home by phone. "Oh, I can't talk to a reporter about the arm-breaking," I told my daughter. "I could get in trouble."

Georgianne asked me how, fifty years later, that there be any retribution for telling my story. I answered that I wasn't supposed to share what happened at Las Piñas in 1944.

When I returned home, I called the reporter to explain the situation. A few days later, the reporter contacted me with a written release from the USMC that I could go public with my story. Within a week's time, I was on TV, demonstrating how I broke my fellow prisoners' arms with the explanation, "I picked up a board and whack!"

Here's my arm breaking story that I can finally share.

They call me an amateur medical technician now. This is because I broke 17 arms of fellow POWs while at the Las Piñas work camp located just south of Manila.

It started during a routine discussion while doing picking and shoveling on the airfield the Japanese were building with American POW, Filipino, and Formosan labor. The field was adjacent to the Nichols Field Air Base, and I believe the Japanese wanted this to be an auxiliary field for Nichols.

One of the Marines I routinely worked with was Wolf, one of the younger men. He talked of escape (practically impossible in that area), but I warned him of the dangers. He finally settled on an injury that would put him on the no-work list.

A couple of other POWs had driven a pick through a foot—self-inflicted but "accidental." Such a wound took quite some time to heal due to the lack of medical supplies and treatment. Also, there was a fear of tetanus with these kinds of wounds.

Wolf emphasized that he had enough of forced labor. He said a broken arm would keep him off the work list. He looked at me and said, "Would you break my arm?" I thought one broken arm wouldn't be serious, so I said, "I'll do it."

There were 800 POWs in this camp (way up from the usual 500 in most camps.) The POWs lived in four buildings, each divided into four rooms of fifty POWs each. The Navy and Marines were in the rear building, with the fence being a short distance away. This provided an isolated area behind the buildings, and there were many scraps of 2 X 4's laying under the buildings.

Wolf approached me the next day and reminded me that I had promised to break his arm. I really hadn't meant it when I said I'd break his arm, but Wolf thought otherwise. I said, "OK, bring in a pick handle." There were some blocks on the ground around the barracks I could use, too.

Wolf "limped" in from work using the pick handle as a crutch. That's when I realized he was serious about this. Inside our compound, he told me he had the tools for the arm breaking.

After dark, we went out behind the building. I positioned two pieces of 2 X 4's under his left arm, one near his elbow, the other near his wrist. I asked him again if he were sure about this, and he indicated for me to go ahead. I aimed the pick handle at the middle of his forearm and hit him with a hard blow. His arm seemed to bend from the area I hit. Wolf asked me if the arm were broken, and I told him that it was obvious and that he should "fall down," get some mud on his body, and then report the injury.

That was the beginning but certainly not the end. The word got out, and I was in business almost every night. One night I had a double header. I still don't know why I did this. It was sort of like seeing what I could get away with, and I felt an obligation if asked.

Routinely, the Japanese guards and honchos lined up the sick and disabled at the gate as the POW workers struggled off to work each morning. This was to shame the sick into getting well so they could share the work with their friends. Each morning, a group of POWs with their left arms in slings stood at the gate. Their numbers grew larger each day. Then I broke the right arm of a left-handed sailor (I'll call him "Sky). He lined up with the disabled—sixteen POWs with broken left arms and one with a broken right arm. It was obvious when the proverbial light bulb went off in the guard's head. He had figured it out that the usable arm was never broken.

I was glad when it was over because I was caught up in something that was getting out of hand. Fortunately, there wasn't enough time for the guards to investigate or perhaps they didn't want to pursue it. I'm sure that my head would have met a sword if I'd been discovered.

There is a postscript to my short arm-breaking career. A few years after the war ended, I was a gunnery sergeant aboard the battleship New Jersey in the Brooklyn Navy Yard. I was leaving the yard, when I heard a unique sound that was common in the Philippines. I knew it had to be from a former POW. Looking around, I saw a Navy officer. The man gave me a Filipino hands signal to approach him. The officer was "Sky," the left-handed sailor whose arm I had broken at Las Piñas. After saying hello, Sky informed me that he was in the Brooklyn Naval Hospital. "You son-of-a-bitch," he said. "This is the third time I've been in the hospital to have my arm rebroken and reset. Thanks, George." Such gratitude.

My construction career wasn't as legendary. Building a runway in rice paddies is difficult if not impossible. The paddies had to be drained with very poor equipment. Survey stakes were "accidentally" moved, and the path of the runway was deliberately not level. However, after several months, the first short part of the runway was completed. This runway consisted of a concrete veneer over a thin layer of crushed coral rock. This was built on top of drained rice paddies. Remember that the concrete was mixed by hand by the prisoners, and we may or may not have mixed it to specifications. Also, the Japanese engineers decided not to pack the ground under the runway to create a solid foundation.

Ceremonies planned to celebrate the opening of the runway were delayed for several days because of a tropical storm. When the celebratory day arrived, several Japanese officials attended the event and lined up along the runway with the prisoners to watch the first landings and take-offs. A Japanese Zero approached the runway and made a "touch and go" run without coming to a stop with the background shouts of "*Banzai*!"

Since the Zero eventually landed safely, a larger, heavier twin engine made its appearance. A Japanese VIP was aboard. All seemed to be a normal landing as the plane landed and began its roll-out to stop. As the plane slowed, the wheels went through the concrete veneer of the runway and became stuck. I'm not saying that we could take all the credit for what happened. A lot of the fault was poor planning by the Japanese. However, it was very satisfying.

Life in Las Piñas continued to deteriorate. It was obvious that the war wasn't going well for Japan, and rations were getting smaller and smaller in the spring and summer of 1944. Some days, the vegetable ration for the 800 men in the camp would total a dozen small squash. The rice sacks were always short, and the prisoners often had fewer than 500 grams of rice daily. Men in the field picked any edible weeds or grass, and small animals and insects disappeared. At least two drums of rancid coconut oil used for lubrication disappeared and was used by prisoners as cooking oil, and a few of my fellow bunkmates cooked large rats daily in the confiscated coconut oil. Some men even ate monkeys, but I drew the line at that. Monkeys looked too much like children. Those overinflated thousands of pesos that had been smuggled into the camp were almost worthless. Coconuts sold for 25 centavos (.02 each prewar), duck eggs were 12 centavos (1941 - .05 each), and peanuts cost 80 centavos a kilo (prewar - .10). The money was worthless, and the prisoners were starving.

This starvation didn't only affect us, as civilians were starving, too, and POWs in other camps shared our fate. The Bilibid staff was placed on 250 grams of rice and corn daily. Cabanatuan's rations were also reduced, and the Japanese did not allow any civilian assistance. The guards at Cabanatuan had finally uncovered the channels through which notes, information, money, and food had been smuggled into the camp. Regulations and punishment at all POW camps were becoming even more severe.

It was very obvious that the momentum of the war had shifted. Supervisors became more impatient and mean. We worked in groups of fifty and when work was finished for the night, we fell into formation. The guards enjoyed opening ranks, grabbing pick handles, and telling us to work harder tomorrow.

The prisoners knew not to show any emotion, but we were past that stage. Our psychology was if the guard injured us, we couldn't work. If we were killed, that was the end. If we weren't hurt, we'd be back tomorrow. That summarized life behind barbed wire. Another new method of punishment was introduced which was being beaten until welts appeared on the prisoners' legs. We soon realized this situation couldn't go on forever. We couldn't escape, but we were wearing down. We had to hold on until the Americans returned and by this time, we had been prisoners for more than thirty months.

I believe we were kept alive for one purpose only – to work. To keep us going, we got the same food every day – a ration of rice and weed soup. I worked for more than a year in just a straw hat and a G-string and barefoot,

Yes, it was tough, but our courage never lessened nor our faith in America questioned. Like all good Americans, it was our collection of courage and spirit which ultimately helped us to survive and prevail in life and death over our captors. We just had to hang on.

We knew that we couldn't escape, so we had fun tormenting our guards. Las Piñas was guarded by some of the meanest bunch of people in the Japanese Army in my opinion. I was beaten more than once for absolutely no reason. The guards were sadistic and brutal so in an attempt to dehumanize them, we gave them nicknames. One guard was called "Porky Pig" because he grunted and look like a pig. He was as mean as a wild boar, and we stayed out of his way. He was very sadistic and as it became apparent that Japan was losing the war, our treatment became worse.

Another memorable guard was "Timex." He loved watches and had the prisoners promise him that we would send him watches when we returned to the U.S. I didn't follow up on that and doubt if any of us did.

"Blinky" was an older man who was a guard at Palawan. You can guess how he earned his name. "Blinky" certainly wasn't at the top of his class. His favorite game was having us guess how many fingers would be used to slap another person's wrist. I tended to burst out laughing when "Blinky" lost and wound up with a red wrist from being slapped. "Blinky" was harmless if a bit slow, and we later learned that he had been injured when the Japanese invaded the Philippines. He became more like a gentle and lovable pet to us. Some men wanted to take advantage of "Blinky" and try to escape, but no one did.

We labeled one guard "Donald Duck." The prisoners there knew him well because he watched us as we worked on the never-ending airfield construction. "Donald" was a moronic-acting man who usually perched himself on high ground above the sweating POWs, chanting threats and curses, demanding us to work harder. The name "Donald Duck" was perfect for him. He closely copied the cartoon Donald with his squawking and screaming. When he realized that we were calling him "Donald," he demanded to know the meaning of his new nickname. We assured him that Mr. Donald Duck was a great movie star who was idolized by millions of adoring Hollywood fans.

Immediately, "Donald" changed. He became nicer and friendlier and began to brag to his fellow soldiers that he was destined for Hollywood stardom when the Emperor's soldiers conquered the United States. A few weeks later, the tranquil mood of "Donald" abruptly ended. Donald had returned to his old, contemptuous self. What had happened to break the peace? The night before, the Japanese had received a shipment of American films. Yes, Donald Duck was featured in one of the films and no, our guard was not amused.

I had been a prisoner-of-war for thirty months by September 1944. Every day was the same. We were just surviving.

The prisoners at Las Piñas were at work as usual on the morning of September 21, 1944. The Filipinos had been optimistic for several days because there had been news that Americans were bombing the southern islands. The air raid sirens in Manila had sounded often in the past few days, but there had been no raids. The sky was full of planes, but no bombs had fallen.

We were on one end of an unfinished runway, going through the motions of working, remarking as planes took off from another runway. One of the planes we were watching—a twin-engine attack bomber—burst into flames and headed to the ground as the report of gunfire was heard. We wondered why the Japanese were shooting down their own planes. Suddenly, it became apparent that many of those planes were not Japanese but were American Navy fighters and dive bombers. We had waited almost three years for this, and we were enjoying it.

After several hours of dive bombing and strafing by the American pilots, Nichols Field was burning and exploding. A squadron dived on the runway where the prisoners were working, grazing some Formosans. Soon the sky was cleared of Japanese planes, and the American pilots turned towards Manila Bay. By the next morning, the ships docked at Manila Bay were bombed. The bamboo telegraph reported that thirty-eight ships had been sunk in Manila Bay.

I was struck in the leg with shrapnel during the initial American air raid, but I was so excited about seeing our planes and didn't realize that I was bleeding. I was yelling at the planes and shouting, "That damn pilot had ham and eggs for breakfast! All I had was that damn rice!"

The prisoners wanted to believe that their liberation was soon. We thought it couldn't be long now. Then we were told we were going to Japan. The worst was before us.

Chapter Fourteen

Living in Hell

"As the anchor chain comes up, the ship's winches start tightening down the hatch covers so that there will be no escape except only through eight torpedo-made holes in the side of the ship. If anyone believes in the philosophy of being the most interested spectator at your own funeral (the idea that your spirit will be watching), I can tell you what a coffin lid sounds like when it goes in place. It will sound like a ship's hatches closing and the winches securing and pulling cables over them. You become helpless... but you are still competing to live."

George Burlage

As strong as the will to survive is, sometimes survival requires more than just will. It is a matter of fate.

In the fall of 1944 as the American forces approached the Philippines, prisoners-of-war were being shipped to Japan to work as slave laborers for Japanese companies. The men were stuffed into the holds of rusty, filthy ships, hatches were shut, and panic began below the decks as the men were plunged into darkness. Little water and food were provided, and many of the men began to slip into madness. American planes and submarines, not knowing

that the ships contained Allied prisoners, attacked the convoys, killing thousands.

George Burlage sat in the hold of the Hokusen Maru for almost forty days, contemplating his fate, fighting off crazed men, and trying to survive. He began to doubt the oath that he had sworn to himself at Corregidor, the oath that he would survive. What happened on his hell ship was something that he could not control. He just had to wait it out and hope.

The prisoners' hope for freedom and release after the American invasion of the Philippines quickly ended. The Japanese military was planning to transport the men to Japan for companies to use as slave laborers. The military was handing over custody of the prisoners to Mitsubishi, Kawasaki Heavy Industries, Mitsui, Nippon Steel, Showa Denko, and other companies because the military couldn't afford to keep us any longer. The American pilots had visited Manila recently, and Manila Bay was a graveyard of ships. There weren't many ships left that could make it to Japan. Nevertheless, on the afternoon of October 1, 1944, the POWs from Las Piñas were taken to Pier 7 at Manila to await transportation. The destruction of the piers was evident, and I wondered how the Japanese would find us transport.

Other groups of prisoners from various camps arrived to join the wait on the pier behind the once beautiful Manila Hotel. Late afternoon, a freighter smaller than 3000 tons pulled alongside. A ship that was old and had been used to carry coal crept in and stopped at the pier. The hatches were uncovered, and we were ready to load. I remember thinking that this wouldn't be too bad and that we would probably be put on the deck for the trip. I then learned that more than 1000 of us were going to make the trip on the *Hokusen Maru* not in cabins or even on the deck. We were being shoved into the ship's hold. We soon renamed the ship "the Horror Maru." Another name given to the ship was "Benjo Maru." That name literally translates as "Shit Ship." On a previous journey, horses had been transported in the hold along with coal.

The after hold was loaded first, and then my group of six hundred was sent below deck into a space of what I estimated to be forty- by-fifty feet in size. The first men lined the bulkhead shoulder to shoulder, and the next row's backs touched the first row's chests. This was the pattern until the hold was filled.

We had been issued winter clothing for Japan. The heat in the hold was suffocating, and many of the men who wore the heavier clothing passed out. The prisoners complained about the heat and the conditions, and the guards answered that the men would be crowded in the hold only to Corregidor in Manila Bay. A larger ship would meet their ship there to take the prisoners to Japan.

The guards covered the hatch with planks, the cover was tied down with wire rope, and then the cover was secured with a winch. If you want to know when competition begins, let your captors push you into the hold of a ship, standing back to breast, tropic heat, no water, and head that unmarked ship out to sea in submarine infested waters.

Conditions in the hold were brutal. It was suffocatingly hot in that hold, and we were at the pier for three days. Soon we had room to sit down because so many men had died. The horses that had been transported on the *Hokusen Maru* along with coal left the floor of the hold covered with coal dust and manure. The stench was horrible, and it was almost impossible to breathe. The coal was useful, though for relieving yourself. The guards lowered food buckets and a "honey" bucket (for waste) a few times a week. They also lowered ropes to tie around the dead to be raised to the deck and thrown overboard.

A form of *Dante's Inferno* quickly developed in the hold. No water, tropical heat, pushing, clawing, trampling, biting, and screaming filled the hold. The guards threatened to shoot the prisoners if they didn't become quiet. Zombie-like men wandered the hold, crazed by thirst. They would fall over other men, and many of these "zombies" would be kicked to death. This all happened before we had even left the pier. It is difficult to fully describe the horror of that hold.

The convoy left Manila after three days at the pier. There were around twenty ships in the convoy, accompanied by five escorts. The voyage was estimated to last twelve days. The men thought that once the ship sailed, they would be transferred to a larger ship. Instead, the ship would be our home—a death ship— for thirty-eight days.

I truly doubted if this ship would make it to Japan. None of the ships were marked as carrying prisoners-of-war, a Geneva Accords and International Red Cross violation. Aboard the *Hokusen Maru* were two hundred Dutch and British POWs. They were the only survivors out of 1,200 prisoners who had been traveling on another hell ship. The ship had been attacked and sunk by American torpedo planes on September 21. We POWs were aware that there was a very good chance that we would die at sea—bombed by Americans. (Six ships in the 38-ship convoy eventually reached Japan.)

"Is this hell? Have I died and gone to hell?" was my constant thought as I sat in the stifling, unrelenting heat in the hold. The horse manure smell was sickening, but since I had eaten almost nothing for days, I couldn't vomit. We couldn't sweat due to dehydration. I began licking the condensation from the inside hold to obtain some sort of moisture. I was just so thirsty, so parched. Crazed men were attacking other prisoners, hitting them with their empty canteens or sometimes urinating in the canteen to make them heavier, then using the canteen as a club. Men tried to climb up the ladder to the deck to escape but, of course, didn't succeed. We went days without water or food and when the rope was lowered with whatever our guards decided to feed us or give us water (never enough), men fought to get to the ropes first, trampling others and causing injuries. I was watching a horror movie with Zombie-like men desperate with thirst and hunger in real time. The hold was dark, so I watched the movement of the shadows and crawled farther away from what was happening.

This was a new situation for me, something that I had not experienced in this thirty-plus months of confinement. I was helpless and couldn't attempt to be one step ahead of or to outsmart my captors. I was trapped in the bottom of a ship, the hold covered by planks and winches, in the South China Sea. Bombs were falling around our ship, and we could hear the torpedoes. My hope was that if my ship were hit, my death would be quick. Still, I had thought out an escape plan in case my ship was bombed and planned to manage to make my way out of the ship and swim for help. Later, I learned of the fate of other POWs who were on the hell ships. An estimated 126,000 Allied prisoners-of-war were placed on 134 hell ships. Casualties were approximately 21,000. One-third of Allied POWs who died in captivity lost their lives aboard a hell ship. Japanese guards often killed prisoners attempting to escape from a sinking ship.

On the third day out, the ship was rocked by a loud explosion which rocked the ship and filled the hold with gas fumes. Our imaginations ran wild, but there wasn't a sound within the hold. We all awaited death. Immediately, there were two more explosions, and then the Japanese ships were dropping depth charges. Three of the ships in the convoy had been sunk.

We all prayed that when we were hit, it would be over quickly. The suspense was terrible. We were sure we were going to be attacked, and explosions were sporadic for several days. I was sitting next to a chief who had some sea experience and was a longtime acquaintance. "George," the chief said, "We're going to get hit by a torpedo."

I asked him how he knew that. He answered, "I heard some knocking off the hold last night." I answered that the chief didn't know how sonar sounded and as the chief finished his explanation, the ocean was booming outside the hull, and subs were sinking everything all around us. The convoy hugged the coast to prevent attacks, but the ploy didn't work. We could hear torpedoes whizzing around us and sonar echoing off the hull. We sat in the coffin -like darkness, and we were helpless.

On October 7, the remaining ships in the convoy docked at Lappoc Bay. After learning of American submarine activity around Formosa, the convoy split in half. We were not allowed out of the hold. On the approach to Formosa, two more ships were sunk. The *Hokusen Maru* captain began a zig-zag course and going in large circles, hoping to prevent an attack.

By October 11, four of the remaining ships arrived in Hong Kong. After docking, the guards allowed the prisoners to go up on deck for a few minutes. They led us up to walk the deck, and then we were put back in the hold. We were in that hold for thirty-eight days, and that was the only time we were out of the ship.

I knew we were in Hong Kong because I had been through there before the war. The ships were several hundred miles off course due to the submarine attacks. The Japanese were unsure of their moves, and the ships were anchored at Hong Kong for ten days while the ships' captains planned their next moves. The prisoners were kept captive in the hold during the entire time. During the ten days, the prisoners argued with our guards because we couldn't understand why the Japanese wouldn't just leave us in Hong Kong. It was apparent that we would never get through the submarine blockade in the China Sea.

Conditions in the hold completely deteriorated during those ten days at anchor. Thirst-crazed prisoners were killing one another in attempts to alleviate thirst. I talked with a medic in the tomb of the hold, and he shared that he had a vial of morphine. He offered to split it with me "to make things easier." By this point in the nightmarish situation, some prisoners were attempting to bite other men's throats for a taste of blood to ease thirst.

I thought for a few seconds and then asked the medic, "How are things different for you than for anyone else in this mess?" I declined the offer of morphine. "I think that I will just stick around and see how this turns out," was my answer. I was really curious to see what else could happen. I had made it this far, and I certainly wanted to find out how this nightmare ended. I also needed to stay alert if I had any chance of survival. The medic swallowed the entire contents of the vial, taking his own life.

On the seventh day we were anchored in Hong Kong, bombers returned, and a bunch of four-motor bombers and dive-bombers attacked the dock area as we were lying in that hold, looking up through the cracks in the cover. We watched those planes come right over our ship and could see the Chinese Air Force markings on the American-made planes.

The ships remained in port for two more days, and on the tenth day, the Japanese ordered the ships to start for Formosa. By this time, most of the hysteria had calmed down because, truthfully, only the stronger men were still alive. Ten days later, the ship dropped anchor at the port of Takao on the southwest coast of Formosa (Taiwan.) We were still imprisoned on the ship for several more days because the Japanese guards had no instructions. We learned that the port was heavily damaged by American attacks, and we also heard that only a few ships remained in our convoy.

Finally, a date to disembark the ship was set, but on that morning a warning siren was heard. Immediately, the hatch was covered and lashed securely, and the ship put out to sea. I will truthfully say that not one of us expected to return to Formosa because we knew that the American Navy had a task force in that area. The ship was not hit, and during the night, the *Hokusen Maru* returned to the harbor. The next morning, the prisoners were allowed to go ashore.

It had taken thirty-eight days under the most inhumane conditions to get us that far. We were 1,000 miles from Manila. Six out of our thirty-six-ship convoy had survived the attacks and sinkings en route.

I couldn't walk or stand up when attempting to leave the ship. I had no water or food for weeks, so I guess I was living on reserve. My estimate was that I weighed little more than one hundred pounds, almost half of my prewar weight. It took forever for those of us who were left to get off the ship because we had difficulty moving.

It was a warm, beautiful day in Takao, but we couldn't get any farther than the dock. I just fell in the sand right off the side of the dock and remained there for a day. We also got some water and a little food. That night, the march to the train station took longer than planned because we were so weak. Before boarding the train, the Japanese guards sprayed the prisoners' feet with disinfectant, and we were forced to listen to a UCLA graduate, now Japanese interpreter, lecture the men about their situation and future. We were being taken to the northern part of the island.

After leaving the train the next morning, the prisoners were forced to hike to their next camp. The guards told us that we were to stay in this camp for two months. They kept us busy carrying rocks from one side of a school ground to another, but at least I got some strength back. I also had the opportunity to bathe for the first time since leaving the Philippines almost forty days earlier.

There were stacks of books in the school buildings, and many were printed in English. I grabbed a few to read, but the guards were questioning my motives. After a discussion, the guards took any books that included maps but let me keep the rest. They were afraid that I was planning to escape using the maps as a guide. I was on an island. Where would I have gone?

And so, I started another year. I admit that I meditated about my situation on that hellish trip. Concern and a bit of fatalism had set in among the remaining prisoners. The men had little knowledge of events in the rest of the world. We did know, obviously, that the Americans had invaded the Philippines, but the invasion hadn't helped the prisoners-of-war. Instead of being freed, the surviving prisoners were being taken to Japan to work as slave laborers. The military had contracted the men to work for large Japanese corporations.

I shared these thoughts in a POW Recognition Day speech that I presented in 1988:

"... Come right down to it, all days are beautiful. I'm like the blind person... Beauty is something he or she feels. And in comparison, to other

events in my life, especially that of being a prisoner of war, all days of freedom are things of beauty.

"As the Ex-POW bumper sticker reads, 'Freedom is Happiness.'

"I think that my sentiments echo those of other prisoners of war who spent time in any of the Japanese camps stretching from Java to Manchuria, the stalags of Germany, the camps of North Korea and China, in any of the Hotel Hanoi chain. And let us not leave out these people once held or those still held for political purposes in various parts of the world. We, the Ex-POWs, knew our mission and dangers. Those being held today are the victims of another types of war.

"I said' Freedom is Happiness.' But I still easily recall every negative aspect of my detour from combat through capture and forty months of forced labor until freedom. There was first the lost cause of being militarily strangled, the hunger, as a captive being marched through the streets of occupied Manila, suffocating boxcars, marches, torpedoes and bombed ships... Those are things that never go away.

"I need not tell you that one is never prepared for capture. Never! There are abrupt changes—mentally, you are ashamed for failure to country, family, and friends. Add the physical maltreatment: beatings, starving, work to physical exhaustion, fighting disease, and staying alive only by luck and wit. Then comes Freedom with the trauma of trying to get back into your own society and into employment. A little understanding and help would have gone a long way.

"Just as we did our best, we are assured that the new generations in our Armed Forces will always do their best.

"As for my experience as a POW, I'll say this: every day was the same, today is the same as yesterday, and tomorrow will be the same as today. It is life behind barbed wire."

Before being transported from the Philippines, I managed to send a card to my sister back home in Visalia. It was a form card provided by the Japanese military, and the contents were printed in the *Visalia Times-Delta* in mid-nineteen forty-four:

Breaking a silence that has existed since December 1943, is a prisoner of war postal card message from Cpl. George E. Burlage, USMC, addressed to his sister "Miss Lois Burlage, Route 2, Box 896. This sister has been married since Corporal Burlage was taken prisoner at Corregidor and is now Mrs. David Brase, but Corporal Burlage is probably not aware of that. He is the son of Mr. and Mrs. George S. Burlage of Ivanhoe.

The postal card is on a form printed by the Imperial Japanese Army. Part of it is printed out, and blank spaces are left for insertions and then room is provided for a 50-word message. It informs Corporal Burlage's relatives that he is interned at Philippine Military Prison Camp No. 4. He was formerly interned at Camp No. 10.

"My health is good. Trust all are well at home. Regards and best wishes to all. Keep your chin up, and I will try to continue the same. Take care of the folks at home. Love."

Only four messages have been received from Corporal Burlage since he was taken prisoner by the Japanese.

CHAPTER FIFTEEN

BEGINNING ANOTHER YEAR

"in comparison to other events in my life, especially that of being a prisoner-of-war, all days of freedom are things of beauty."

George Burlage

After more than a month in the hold of the hell ship, the prisoners departed their ship at Takao, Formosa (now Taiwan). Weakened by their ordeal, most collapsed in the warm sun and slept.

The Japanese officials in charge realized that the men had reached the limits of their endurance and decided to allow them to stay in Formosa for several weeks to rest and regain their strength. The prisoners hoped that they would remain in Formosa until the war ended, but the Japanese companies needed labor. Too soon, they were loaded into the Melbourne Maru to complete the journey to Moji, Japan, a journey that had begun in Manila months earlier.

George had been a POW for almost three years. He had survived several camps and a hell ship, hard labor, and tropical heat and disease. Now, he would be working in bitter cold in what was one of the coldest winters in Japanese history.

Nearing the end of our time in Formosa, I really began to feel secure in the belief that the war was coming to an end. We thought that we wouldn't be moved again because of the close proximity of the American forces. However, on January 12, 1945, we were informed we were going to Japan, leaving by train in the morning to board ships. We arrived at Takoa where the harbor looked like a burned over forest with the mass of sunken ships sticking out of the water.

The military could no longer keep us because of the scarcity of food, so a deal was made with Mitsubishi and other Japanese companies to use the POWs as slave laborers. We were to work in a lead/zinc mine in Northern Honshu. I believed this would be my last camp. I would leave as a free man or be executed.

Our ship was the pre-war *Melbourne Maru*. There were 500 American and British prisoners and 500 Japanese soldiers aboard. Even though the ship wasn't crowded, we were placed in the hold with salt, and the collection of moisture on the overhead continuously dripped on us, keeping us wet for the entire voyage. The order was to feed us twice daily, but when the ship's captain saw us, he observed that he had been carrying prisoners all during the war and that none looked as bad as we did. He ordered that we were to be given three meals a day.

The ship headed for the China coast near Amoy (now known as Xiamen) and then hugged the coast to Shanghai. From there, it cut across to Korea and finally into Moji on the island of Kyushu. It was an uneventful voyage until the last day. The convoy dropped a number of depth charges after learning that one ship had been sunk by a submarine attack. We anchored in Moji after twelve days at sea. Soon we would be off the ship – or at least that was our hope. It was so cold, freezing cold, and all of us had spent years in the tropics. Our shabby clothing was no protection, and we were waiting to be taken to a warm building very quickly.

The Japanese women stevedores came the next morning. Before daylight, the hatch cover was torn apart, and the cold wind whipped through the wet hold. We were freezing, even though we were wearing all of our clothes and were wrapped in our one blanket per man. We prisoners had seen death from disease, starvation, thirst, and violence, but we had never faced freezing temperatures before. Now, we were being threatened by hypothermia.

Our morale was high, though, as small crafts were tying alongside, preparing to take us ashore. Everyone was excited because we were confident that our treatment would improve in Japan. We were sure that we'd soon be in a warm railroad station, a nice camp with Red Cross clothing and food, perhaps a hot bath. We dreamed of hot food, hot tea, and hot soup. (Another fact: active military personnel and POWs, according to the Geneva Accord, are not allowed to travel on the same ship.)

The Port of Moji, located on the northern coast of Kyushu, proved not to be the Promised Land or Canaan. We found out that nothing would really change except for the climate. There were the usual formations, counting off, shoving, pushing, and slapping. The guards marched us to the ferry, and we crossed the channel to the southern coast of Honshu. Another agonizing journey was beginning.

This new chapter of being a guest of the Emperor had begun, but our hopes were still high that our conditions would improve. After spending the afternoon marching in the freezing weather, we arrived at what the Japanese military described as "barracks." These temporary "barracks" were nothing more than a cold and bare shack with a dust-covered floor. We huddled together to keep warm, and our evening meal was a single small rice ball.

Around midnight a Japanese officer woke us up and began to speak. His words were familiar. "You men are honorable men. You fought honorably against the undefeatable Japanese soldier," he told us. "For a long time, you have worked hard for the Japanese, sometimes with difficulty, and many of you are now sick."

He continued his speech. "Now we reward you— we take you down to Tokyo— to a hospital and rest camp with Red Cross food and medicines," he said. "The first group will leave immediately." He concluded with the usual warning about obedience of orders and threats of severe punishment. Two hundred names were called, and the men gathered their few belongings and fell into formation. Transportation was limited, so this was the first group to leave. Faint smiles of satisfaction were on the men's faces as they marched to the train station, anticipating a warm coach. The train, of course, was delayed. When it finally arrived, we scrambled for seats. We wound up sitting on one another's feet, rubbing one another in an attempt to stay warm. The train was many hours behind schedule as it lumbered north through Hiroshima, Kobe, Yokohama, and finally Tokyo.

The train station at Tokyo wasn't very impressive. The wood buildings were old and outdated. Big wooden water tubs were placed around the city as a precaution against air raids. The tubs were frozen over and would be useless if Tokyo were attacked. A blanket and overcoat were issued to each prisoner as we waited to travel to our new camp.

Fast streetcars transported us to another part of Tokyo and left us lined up along the tracks to wait for our connection. There was a delay of several hours. The men ran in place and exercised to keep from freezing, and many prisoners had no shoes.

The train finally arrived. The two hundred of us were jammed into a coach that was designed to hold only eighty passengers. Even with so many people crammed into a small space, the coach was still cold. The stench of unwashed bodies was overwhelming, and sanitation was impossible.

We were taken off the train the next morning in another area of Tokyo and then waited several hours for the next train. We now knew that there would be no rest camp or Red Cross but that we were headed to another work camp. We had a new obstacle along with hunger and disease—the frigid cold weather.

Tokyo was very desolate, and everyone seemed to be in a hurry. The residents were like robots and emotionless. A German sailor winked at us POWs, but there were no other acknowledgments.

After another long train ride, we boarded a narrow-gauge railroad. The scenery was isolated, snow-covered land. From the sound of the struggling engine, it was apparent that there was a steep grade. The last part of this four-day train journey ended in a small village of Hosokura, a Mitsubishi company town. From the station, the POWs trudged through the snow to our new camp. We would be here until September 2 —our day of liberation from slavery and starvation when the Allies were victorious.

Chapter Sixteen

The Last Camp

"The camp's rules were all the same, no work, no food."

"I hid my dead friends from the guards. I needed their food rations."
George Burlage

The fourth year of captivity began for George Burlage in northern Japan where he was a slave laborer for Mitsubishi Mining. He held the coveted position of a driller and had earned the respect of the Japanese civilian workers at the Sendai #3 camp.

He was also very cold and very hungry.

Both the Japanese workers and the POWs believed that the war was ending. The civilians were starving, too, and American bombers were frequently attacking Japanese cities. The question was, though, how would the war end. Would the Japanese surrender? Would the Americans invade? Would the prisoners-of-war be executed?

Working in the mine gave George the opportunity to associate with Japanese civilians. He soon recognized that the Japanese were as weary of war as the prisoners were, and he even gave some of

his rations to one of the guards whose wife was pregnant. They were all sharing the same reality of cold, hunger, and anticipation of the war's end.

Now I was a miner. Three hundred prisoners—a mixture of Americans, British, and Dutch—were to work a Mitsubishi lead/zinc mine in Northern Honshu. Although a main supplier for the Japanese war machine, Mitsubishi did its work by hand. There was ore-loading machinery made in Pittsburgh, Pennsylvania, that sat idle (perhaps due to lack of fuel), but we mined the old-fashioned way—drill, blast, shovel.

It was bitterly cold when we arrived at the camp so in the oil drum that was used as a stove, we burned our wooden pillows and some rafters. Soon, we started sneaking coal from the mine. The clothing issue was one old Japanese army uniform. I weighed one-half of my normal weight, but the legs were too short. Once again, being a non-smoker helped me. I traded my cigarette rations for two pairs of wrap leggings to cover my skin from the pants to my cloth shoes.

Our barracks were perched on a hill overlooking the mine, and a road led down to the mine. One hundred workers lived in one barracks, and we could hear the wind whistling through the cracks in the wooden walls. There was little protection against cold or rain. The main center deck was concrete, and on either side were two double wooden decks, one about five feet above the other. This was our sleeping space with the concrete deck to be used as the area for formations and eating. The thin wood walls held up a tarpaper roof. It was obvious that these barracks had been quickly constructed especially for us.

There was absolutely no warmth in the barracks. Our fuel was six small sticks of wood and a basket of coal per day. Dinner was usually a cereal mixture of rice, rolled barley, and milo (a type of malt) accompanied by a cabbage-pumpkin soup. The prisoners received five blankets and a wood pillow. Two friends and I decided to put one blanket on the floor and sleep together under the other blankets. We were still cold but warmer. Lice love these blankets, too.

(In the late 1990s/early 2000s, my church sponsored an annual blanket drive for our city's homeless population. I always purchased blankets to remember our keeping warm under those blankets in Japan.)

A few days after our arrival and adjustment, an official from Mitsubishi spoke to us. After the usual formalities of bowing and saluting, he told us of our "kind" treatment but added that, of course, "you must work." The first group would start work tomorrow, and more men would be added daily. Soon, all were working.

Routine was quickly established. Of course, there was a shortage of food and clothing, and soon there were deaths from hypothermia. Removing bodies was an ordeal. It took six men to carry, drag, or pull the bodies the several miles to the crematorium. One advantage of being on burial detail was the warmth of the crematorium. I identified with the main character in the poem "The Cremation of Sam McGee." The requests for more food for the slave laborers were unanswered until the evening an interpreter informed us that we would be provided with a special treat—curried dog. Most of us were not THAT hungry.

It was obvious that Japan was losing the war. The civilians were starving as were the workers. However, when I learned that one of the guards' wife was pregnant and malnourished, I shared my small rations with him so more food would be available for her. This small act of kindness would not be forgotten by the guard. The guard, whose name was Endo, worked closely with another prisoner and me. Endo was not a fan of Mitsubishi management and was very vocal about it. He was "sick" occasionally and gave his rations to his wife. Mitsubishi changed the ration procedure to "sick" employees' rations. The employees received half rations. Soon, the miners were fed at work, all our meals were consumed on site. No work equaled no rice.

Comparatively speaking, life was better at Mitsubishi, but we were still hungry. Even the civilians were on strict rations. The daily brutality was gone because we worked together with the civilians in the mine.

I had even climbed up the hierarchy in the POW world by becoming a driller, a respected position to the Japanese.

A typical day for us began at 7:00 a.m. when we walked down our road from our camp to the mine. We were given an hour for lunch and left the mine around 5:00 p.m. to return to our barracks. We had helmets made of hard fiber board or papier mache and individual lamps. My major complaint was that the mines' ceilings were low, and I had to bend down during most of my labor. As in most mines, the men were divided into three groups—drillers, timber men, and car pushers. Of course, a Japanese civilian worker oversaw each group. There was little opportunity to sabotage, but there were other ways we found to hinder production.

I was assigned to be a driller, a very highly ranked position because we handled explosives. Sabotage was rare because of the risk of danger to the slave laborers. However, if I saw a chance for a little mischief, I grabbed it. Japanese workers operated the cars that removed ore from the mine. Except for deliberate slowness and loading the cars, there really was no sabotage opportunity. However, I did find a way to have some fun. I would pull pins from the coupling that connected the cars, and several of the cars would be left behind on the track. When the driver had a full load of ore in the remaining cars, he would begin backing out of the mine. He had no idea that there were empty cars on the track and crashed into them. The Japanese never considered the POWs as capable of sabotage and blamed the crashes on worn out equipment.

The POWs also unwittingly assisted in the Americanization of Japanese youth. At the Mitsubishi mine, one of the POWs discovered some regular road tar. Within hours, most men had some of the tar, chewing away as if it were spearmint gum. We discovered that it did clean our teeth. The next day, it seemed that every boy in the village was chewing tar (boys twelve years and older did some kind of work at the mine). Soon, an order came down: no one would chew tar. Still, chewing gum had been introduced to Japanese youth.

Ever heard of a "goldbrick?" It's a person who invents excuses to avoid work. I found mine at the Mitsubishi mines, and it was my "honcho" Endo.

Out of the 300 POWs who were sent to this north Honshu mine in early 1945, only seven of us were assigned as drillers. I worked with three different honchos who were rotated every ten days so that they wouldn't become chummy with the laborers. Sometimes, I worked one-on-one with the honchos, but it was usually two POWs with one honcho. It depended on the type of drill—one or two men.

The honchos had different personalities. One was an ex-Army sergeant major who had been wounded at Singapore and placed in a reserve unit. He was afraid of being called up, and he did receive that dreaded call a few weeks before the war ended to join the homeland defense force. Preparations were underway for the eventual American invasion. Another honcho was Sato, who was all work and dedication with a paternal approach.

And then there was Endo. Endo was also a reservist, having served in China for a few years. He lived in constant fear of being called back to active duty but never was. His idea was to get through the day without problems.

Two or three months before the war's end, Mitsubishi bent its rule on rotations and assigned Endo to honcho the drilling for an underground medical station. It was mountainous terrain, and the drill site was just off the one street through the small mining town of Hosakura. Endo, I, and a Navy man whose name I don't remember became a permanent three-man drill team for the job.

Endo didn't think kindly of the Mitsubishi management and was especially angered by the "no work, no rice" rule. His wife was pregnant and needed food. As a honcho, Endo moved in slow motion, and we didn't move any faster. He even allowed us to roam through a nearby field to gather vegetation which we boiled at our noon break to supplement our rice. We always shared our rations with him, and he would take some to his wife.

One thing that did go well was he had me walk the two miles in the mine to the supply area (and back) to get the dynamite we used each day. Endo was too lazy to walk four miles. I got good at forging his name on the request chits. The Japanese civilian workers dishing out the explosive supplies never questioned the validity of the chits.

Then one morning, it all hit the proverbial fan. I had leisurely made the trek into the mine, forged my chit for 120 sticks of dynamite, the necessary fuses, and yards of fuse cord. As I turned a corner on the abandoned and isolated mining road, I routinely took to our drilling site, I came face-to-face with a group of Japanese brass. Ranking the group was the commandant of the Sendai POW area, his staff, and the commander of the local POW barracks. The commandant, a colonel, was making a surprise visit to the Mitsubishi POWs.

Initially, the encounter was friendly. I did a big bow to the group and shouted "Ohio." Then the shock of facing a POW with all that dynamite quickly moved toward the punitive. One of the officers pulled a samurai sword, demanding quick justice, but the colonel said, "Not now," and told one of his staff to take me to Endo. He was to get the "whys" of my action and bring us in office hours. The speculation for punishment ranged from beheading, beating, or confinement.

Endo and I did some quick planning for office hours. He had to answer why I wasn't under guard. One of his "super honchos," who we called "Joe Louis" because of his unusual size and dark complexion, shared that he had a solution. He said we would go before the colonel and then he, "Joe," would knock me down three times, the usual punishment. Endo said that wouldn't work because "Joe" wasn't part of the problem.

Endo and I had our plans for office hours. He would tell the colonel that it was merely miscommunication on his part and ambition on my part. He lied a bit, but it worked. He said we went together for the dynamite, but as we came out of the mine, we stopped at the blacksmith shop to get sharpened drill bits. I apparently didn't understand his orders for me to wait. I was eager to get to work, so I went on to the worksite. After a conversation with the colonel (punctuated with a few elaborate bows), the colonel had me taken outside to await his decision. While waiting, I got condolences from two or three fellow POWs.

Endo and I marched into the colonel's office, did our best bows, and stood at attention. Instead of reading off my punishment, the colonel complimented me by telling me what a great and dedicated worker I had been. He commended me for my hard work and suggested that I be given an extra rice ball for my hard work.

I learned a lot about human nature that day. A POW and his enemy found a solution to a common problem in a slave labor camp. Regarding this solution: I'm sure that on this occasion, and on any one of the dozens of times I carried explosives, through the town unguarded, I had the necessary materials to blow up the mining town of Hosakura. I never once considered doing that, though. I didn't even have a match to ignite the explosives.

I accepted that working at Mitsubishi would last until I was either freed or executed. The POWs had heard rumors that all of us were to be killed if there were an American invasion of Japan. We were treated better by the civilian guards than by the military guards in the Philippines. Many of the honchos wanted to learn English, and I wanted to improve my Japanese. Most of the Mitsubishi hierarchy knew that the war was ending with their defeat, and their treatment of us was better than in the Army-run camps. The Japanese were starving, too.

Many of us developed diseases caused by malnutrition. I weighed about one hundred pounds, one-half of my pre-war weight and had beriberi and pellagra.

There was an older Japanese man who worked in the mine. He knew enough English and I knew enough Japanese to communicate. The man was very worried about his son, who was in Manchuria. He had learned that the Russians had entered the war and invaded Manchuria. He also told me that the Americans were winning the war because of "big ships with little airplanes." I think he was describing air raids.

I hadn't lost my sense of defiance even after all I had endured. The mine had a Shinto shrine high above the entrance. The prisoners were forced to stop and pray every morning to the shrine. My morning mantra while facing east to "pray" was to bow and chant a little rhyme that wasn't very polite to Tojo. Although Tojo had resigned from being prime minister a few months earlier, the Japanese guards still held him in high regard.

One morning during my "prayer," I was knocked down and hit in the back of the head with a board. There was a railroad track by the mine. I slid down the track, and the guard kicked me all the way down, me sliding on my stomach. When I finally stopped sliding, I glanced up at the guard. He smiled at me and remarked, "I speak English." I was hurting, but I felt a self-satisfaction in my small act of defiance.

A few months before this, the same guard announced the death of Franklin Roosevelt. His message was unique: "The son-of-a-bitch Roosevelt is dead. Japan will now win the war." We knew nothing about the German surrender a few weeks later. However, we knew that the Americans were winning. Our Japanese guards knew it, too. Those with sons in the military expressed their anxiety, especially if the Allies invaded Japan. We worried about an invasion, too. We were aware that all POWs in Japan would be executed if there were an invasion because the Japanese military worried that we would fight with the Americans. I had lost so much weight and was starving. I doubt if we even had the strength to be in combat although we certainly had the will. The set execution date was November 1.

Work slowed down at the mine in July. No one including the Japanese seemed to care anymore. Everyone was just tired and hungry. During those last few months in Japan, I often reflected about my twenty-seven years on earth and how I ended up in a POW camp. For forty months of my life, I had existed on hope and the will to live. Would that be enough?

The messages from Tokyo to the camp commanders were intercepted by US codebreakers. The messages confirmed that no POWs or civilian internees were to be freed by Allied forces. The Tokyo order read in part: "in any case, it is the aim not to allow the escape of a single one (prisoner), to annihilate them all, and not to leave any traces" (www.mansell.com).

By the spring and summer of 1945, Japan was under heavy bombings. The most recognizable words in Japanese conversations were "B Ne Ju Ku" —B-29. The prisoners never saw a B-29, but we heard them at night. Time dragged on for us with no news other than garbled bits of news from an incoherent fireman. He told us about the activities of the American Navy and Air Force. Betting odds and morale were high among us, and we even had new courage. The Japanese commandant at the camp had frequent midnight rages, charging through the barracks and knocking prisoners down with his saber. The commandant was quite angry the day he discovered that we had burned all our wooden pillows in an effort to stay warm. It was impossible to know what punishment he would have imposed if he had known that the wooden supports, some of the rafters, and parts of the toilets had also been burned.

As I shared earlier, Mitsubishi was the best camp that I was in because the guards were civilians. One honcho promised me salt for Independence Day. I couldn't remember the last time I had tasted salt, and I craved it. The morning of the Fourth, he appeared in a military uniform and was in tears when he told me, "They called me up, but I don't know why. We've lost the war."

I asked him where he was being sent, and he answered he had been assigned to a beach defense. He then looked at me, tears in his eyes, and said, "No salt. No salt. I'm sorry."

On August 7, the day after Hiroshima was bombed, Navy bombers attacked and destroyed the Mitsubishi mine. The planes dropped through a break in the overhanging clouds and blasted the smelter and powerplant out of commission. We were on our way to work when the bombs struck. The usual morning prayer to the Shinto gods was ignored as we ran for shelter in the mines. We never learned about Japanese casualties. We could hear the bombs hitting outside. I became a bit frightened and thinking, "Well, somebody's wife or daughter was just killed." We left when the bombing ended and found the nearby town was very quiet and calm. I could hear some crying, but most people were just stunned or sitting on the ground. Nobody said a word to us.

A few days later, we returned to the mine to begin salvaging the equipment because there was no way to replace machinery. We worked there two or three days. One afternoon, someone came running into the mine and talked to a guard. The guard then turned to speak to a honcho. I said to a friend, "Something is happening. They're speaking too fast for me to catch it all, but it's obvious this is big." A bit later, the laborers were summoned to the big underground office, lined up, and were joined by other groups. The honchos came in, bowed, and prayed. We learned that the war had ended.

We still weren't sure what this meant for us, so we went back to our barracks. We didn't work for two days. After three days, I went to the interpreter and told him, "We're tired of sitting around. We want to go back to work."

"No work. No work," was the answer. A guard overheard me and said, "Americans, Japanese, friends now. We shake hands."

A day later, both the camp commandant and interpreter disappeared. They had been summoned to Yokohama for instructions about how to handle the POWs. Upon his return to Sendai, the commandant, who spoke English, asked to speak to all the men. "I have been to Yokohama and now have instructions from your friends.

"The war is over. We will feed you, make you fat and healthy. You will be going home to your wives, friends, and mothers." He took his sword, handed it to his captain and left.

Our immediate reaction was, "How do we get out of here." Discipline didn't break down, and we followed rules and regulations. All the guards disappeared. The Americans enjoyed a Scottish soldier who found an American flag and took it to the British barracks. When he walked into the barracks, he instructed the British, "All right, let's salute it. The Americans won the war for us." He told us later he wanted to move to the United States when he was released.

We stayed at the camps for a few weeks. One prisoner had an old Japanese radio, and he located an Armed Forces Radio station. The announcer was instructing POWs to stay where we were and await freedom. The food drops killed three prisoners because the parachutes weren't the right kind for the heavy loads, and some of the metal barrels actually hit people. The first outsider who came to the camp was from the Swedish Embassy and was accompanied by an Army combat reporter. The Swede told us, "There aren't Americans on the island yet, so you'll need to stay here." We waited and waited. We ate the provided food, took vitamins, and learned about penicillin use. We felt good in our new khakis, waiting for the word to leave.

Three weeks after August 15, after the official surrender in Tokyo Bay, we marched out of our camp as proud Americans in our new, clean khaki uniforms, heads held high. We went from the mountain and mine to Sendai, a large city on Honshu. Sendai is near the coast, and a fleet from Alaska had just arrived. We commandeered a little gauge railroad that Mitsubishi had built and traveled two or three hours to the main line. After boarding the big train, I saw a Japanese man wearing a green armband with "tourist guide" printed on it. I looked at him and said, "What kind of business are you in?" He answered, "Before the war, I was a tourist guide. There'll be lots of Americans here now." He was taking the situation in stride.

When we arrived at Sendai, the Navy was ready to take us to the ships. The Navy drivers only had one speed— wide open— as we went down the streets. When we arrived at the dock, I had my first post-POW disappointment. The officials overseeing the released prisoners checked me over on the hospital ship, labeled me as "malnourished," and sent me to a British destroyer. I was drinking hot tea and eating hardtack when I glanced over to a nearby American ship. "Hey, you SOBs!" I shouted. "You're eating ice cream while I'm stuck with hardtack!" I craved anything that was cold, but the British only had warm drinks and food.

When we arrived at Tokyo Bay, the massive display of American strength and might was impressive. My last memory of American forces was bombed airfields, Pearl Harbor, and surrender. As far as I could see, American ships filled the bay. While I was in prison camp, the United States had fulfilled its promise to indeed be "the arsenal of democracy." Finally, aboard an American ship, I asked for cold chocolate milk. My stomach had shrunk during my captivity, and I couldn't keep down the milk. I threw up, then asked for another glass of milk. I didn't care that I couldn't keep it down. I just wanted that sensation of cold milk.

I finally had my first plane experience when I was flown from Tokyo to the US Navy hospital on Guam. Ice cream was provided for patients, and it was so cold and so wonderful. I had been craving ice cream, milk, and cold beer for forty months. At the Guam Hospital, one of my POW friends "borrowed" a few gallons of ice cream for us to enjoy. No one said anything to us and allowed us to enjoy our treat.

After a short time on Guam, we were taken to Hawaii for more examinations and then on to Oakland for a four-month stay at the naval hospital there. I could leave, though, so I had the opportunity to travel the two hundred miles to my hometown, Visalia, to visit with my family. So much had changed in my six-year absence. Both of my sisters were married with families, and my mother's health had declined (she died in 1948). I did reunite with my brother Robert after 8 ½ years. He had served in the Pacific during the war.

I was taunted by some men in Visalia who accused me of cowardice because I was captured. For a while, I told people that I had worked in an aircraft factory during the war due to the absence of understanding of what I had endured.

While in Visalia, I met my oldest niece who was five years old. She stared at me, arms crossed, and seriously looked at me. "Why are you so skinny?" she asked. "You are so tall but so skinny."

It would take me while to regain my weight, but I did—with some extra pounds added on.

Forty months of hard labor, drudgery, malnutrition, disease, and uncertainty were over for me. I was finally at home.

Chapter Seventeen

Restarting Life

"When I visited the site of one of my POW camps, I said two prayers. One prayer was for God to forgive my Japanese captors for their cruel and inhumane treatment of their prisoners.

"My other prayer was for myself that before I leave this earth, I can forgive my captors."

Conversation with a former American prisoner-of-war (Georgianne Burlage, 2018, American Defenders of Bataan and Corregidor—Memorial Society convention)

After forty months as a prisoner of the Japanese, George Burlage was free. He had regained control of his life and his future and had fulfilled his oath made on Corregidor. He had survived.

Now he had decisions to make. He also needed to catch up with events of the past forty months and with his family. His sisters had both married and had children. His brother, who also had served in the Pacific, was staying in the Navy. His mother's health was declining.

George knew that he wasn't ready to return to college. He was restless, and he was receiving medical treatment for his tropical

diseases. He really didn't know where and how to begin to start the rest of his life. He began by re-enlisting in the Marine Corps which led to travel and eventually to his journalism career. The "romance" that was promised on the recruiting poster in 1939 came true when he married in 1950. In 1959, he retired from the Marines after twenty years of service and completed his college education and settled into life as a civilian.

My forty months as a prisoner-of-war were like pressing the pause button on a video recording. My life was paused in December 1941, and the play button was pressed in September 1945.

First, I needed rehabilitation. That required six months in and out of the Naval hospital at Oakland, California. I visited my family in Visalia a few times, but everything was different. I was restless and tired of justifying my capture. People wanted to know how I "got myself caught," and I began saying that I worked in an aircraft factory during the war.

My long-range goal was to finish college, but I accepted that I was not physically or mentally 100 percent. While at Oakland, I asked many times to speak to a counselor. My answer was "to go home and eat a home-cooked meal with your family." That's what I did, and my mother helped me with my decision to stay in the Marines. Her advice was that I had missed out on the war by being a POW and believed that I should re-enlist with the goal of traveling and recovering from my experiences. I could complete college later.

In May 1946, I was assigned to the Marine Corps Pacific headquarters in San Francisco, but my tenure there was short. In a few months, I was aboard the *USS New Jersey*. While serving on the *New Jersey*, I asked if I could write articles about the Marines on the ship to be submitted to their hometown papers. I received permission, and that's when my writing talent was discovered. After my return to the States when my tour was over, my Marine life would take a drastic turn.

My *New Jersey* voyage began in Bremerton, Washington. From there, we sailed south through the Panama Canal to Bayonne, New Jersey. After picking up 600 midshipmen and Navy ROTC cadets at Annapolis, we headed across the Atlantic to Scotland, Oslo, and Portsmouth and then back to Guantánamo Bay, Cuba. After a few weeks in Cuba, I returned to the Brooklyn Navy Yard and was assigned to recruiting duty in Altoona, Pennsylvania. I spent two months recruiting, but no one joined. The war was over. All most men cared about was enjoying the peace.

The fall of 1947, I was sent to Great Lakes, Illinois, to attend the Naval School of Journalism, a twelve-week course designed by Northwestern University. I graduated at the top of the class and was assigned to the USMC public affairs office in D.C. From there, I was sent to be the writer and photographer for the Sixth Fleet in the Mediterranean. Six months were spent traveling in North Africa and the East Mediterranean area, writing stories about individual Marines to publicize the Corps. I filed 6,500 news releases to various media outlines.

After my return to the States, I joined the staff at the West Coast office of *Leatherneck Magazine* and was based in San Francisco. While stationed on the West Coast, part of my duties was to be the official Marine advisor for two World War II – themed movies, *Halls of Montezuma* and *Flying Leathernecks.* I never met John Wayne, though.

In January 1950, I was visiting my hometown in Central California when a high school friend set me up on a blind date with her teaching colleague. The woman's name was Willie Mae Donnelly, a Texan who had moved to California to teach. After four dates, I proposed to her. "You're going back to Texas for the summer," I said to her. "We like each other, and we aren't going to do any better. Let's get married."

Willie Mae said that she had to think about it. "Tell you what," I answered. "I'll drive by your apartment in the morning at 9:00 a.m. If you are waiting outside, we'll get married. If you're not, I have enjoyed knowing you."

She was waiting for me. We eloped in Las Vegas over Memorial Day in 1950. When her school year was over, we moved to San Diego where Willie Mae was hired in a nearby district. Soon, the Korean Conflict began, and *Leatherneck* sent me to South Korea as a combat correspondent where I was for almost two years. While in Asia, I traveled to the Philippines to write an article about the tenth anniversary of the Fall of Corregidor. I also went to occupied Japan. Both trips were very bittersweet, not nostalgic.

In 1952, we moved across the country when I was transferred to Philadelphia to serve as public information chief for the Northeastern Recruiting Area. After three years in that position, it was time to return to the "real" Marine Corps. I was assigned as the chief of the public information office for the 2nd Marine Division at Camp Lejeune, North Carolina. A future governor of and senator from Georgia, Zell Miller was part of my staff. Our daughter, Georgianne, was born at Camp Lejeune in 1955. We were fortunate that Willie Mae always found a teaching position anywhere I was stationed. She taught in Camden, New Jersey, across the Delaware River from Philadelphia and at Jacksonville, North Carolina, High School after Georgianne was born.

While at Lejeune, I went to Turkey to cover Operation Deep water. The maneuvers were at Gallipoli, a famous World War I battle site. I had always enjoyed the Sixth Fleet maneuvers, but becoming a father changed my mind about being gone for weeks. I began to consider retiring when I completed twenty years in the Corps.

Kaneohe Bay, Hawaii, was my last duty station. I left Camp Lejeune in May 1958 to be the chief of the combined MCAS-brigade public information office. However, I was assigned as editor of the *Winward Marine*, the weekly newspaper serving the Marines on Oahu. This was an experience-filled job which I enjoyed. Again, Willie Mae secured a teaching position at a local high school, and Georgianne attended nursey school on the Kaneohe Base. We were living in Hawaii when it became a state, and that was a memorable celebration.

I left the service August 31, 1959, after 20 years and 45 days as a Marine. Feeling rich with a $185 monthly retirement pension and a $150 G.I. Bill college payment each month, I enrolled at what is now the University of North Texas to complete my college education that I had started in 1937 back in Visalia. I chose North Texas because it was Willie Mae's alma mater, and we would be near her family. I also was a reporter for the *Denton Record-Chronicle* while at North Texas and soon became its regional editor. I graduated from UNT in 1960, and three years later, I became the public affairs officer for the Southwestern Region of the Federal Aviation Administration in 1963. In 1969, I earned my master's degree in public affairs from UNT.

After forty years of being an employee of the United States government (twenty in the Marines, twenty at FAA), I retired. Retirement turned out to be anything but retiring as I have been busy with volunteer activities, veterans' causes, and my two granddaughters. I have had the opportunity to travel to Atlanta, New York City, Maine, and Washington, D.C., where I attended the dedication of the World War II Memorial.

Those forty months behind barbed wire were decades ago, and I have had a full life with two careers, a family, and education, and many, many experiences. I have often wondered, though, how I survived when so many didn't. The estimate is that only 60 percent of us who were captured by the Japanese survived. I cheated death so many times by getting off Palawan, somehow beating malaria, not getting caught for breaking arms, by being in the right hell ship, and by good decisions—and a whole lot of luck.

I survived my captivity malnourished but in relatively good health. The tropical diseases and vitamin deficiencies did affect my digestive tract, and my family doctor believes that my later-in-life osteoporosis may have been caused by my POW camp diet. I had malaria relapses, but those decreased over time. I was fortunate that probably my only "souvenir" from being a POW was claustrophobia resulting from the hell ship experience and working in the mine. Still, how did I survive?

I was healthy when captured. I had grown up on a farm and was strong from physical labor. My mind stayed healthy, and I wouldn't allow despair to envelop me. Most of the men who instantly gave up hope when captured at Corregidor didn't make it through the war. I swore when captured that I would survive and always tried to be one step and one thought ahead of my guards. My body was strong, my mind was healthy, and I had a good outlook... and again lots of luck. That's why I survived. No one was going to rob me of my future.

Can the story of a prisoner-of-war of any war really be told? In the Pacific Theater in World War II, thousands of military personnel and civilians spent several years with their captors. We came home for the most part unnoticed, many of us hitchhiking home. Our treatment was minor; our doctors instructed us to go home to our mom's cooking. Some former POWs were accused by military purists of being cowards. These "purists" failed to realize that the actions leading to a personal surrender involve physical contact with the enemy.

From the first day of my captive life, I had confidence that I would make it. I had to live one day at a time, knowing that today and tomorrow would be a repeat of yesterday, but that every day was one day closer to freedom. How did I survive? It wasn't due to Red Cross packages as we never received any (the Japanese kept them for themselves). My survival was due to sheer will, not giving up, and accepting the challenge of being a prisoner-of-war. I had faith in myself and in my nation.

It was difficult. My experiences were hard to discuss and even harder to explain. I had witnessed torture, execution, and brutality. I was on a hell ship for 38 days without light and little water and food and watched my friends die one by one. I worked in a coal mine. I was a slave laborer for the Imperial Japanese Army. This was difficult for people to understand. My mother advised me to re-enlist in the Corps. That's what I did, and it saved me.

I had survived while most did not. I had sworn to myself when I was captured that I would make it through whatever was ahead of me as a prisoner-of-war, and I fulfilled that promise

No blueprint or rules exist for survival. There is no road map to get you from sunrise to sunset. What you did today to stay alive could get you killed tomorrow. I had to explore my emotional and physical path each day and start over daily. If I were successful, I lived. If not, I died.

I started my new life as a prisoner-of-war by stealing a canteen of water from a Japanese guard. Psychologically, I outsmarted him. Physically, I needed that water to survive. I tried to outwit my captors whenever possible. I stole beer on Palawan. I moved stakes while helping to build an airstrip at Las Pinas to guarantee that any plane that arrived would have a rough landing because the runway was uneven. I broke arms of fellow prisoners so that they wouldn't have to work. When I got caught reading textbooks in an abandoned school, I talked my way out of the danger. The textbook was full of maps, and my guards believed that I was planning to escape. I told them I loved being with them and had no desire to leave. They believed that lie. I couldn't escape. I was in Asia, and I had blonde hair and blue eyes. I would be spotted in a second.

One situation that was more pure luck that I survived than outsmarting guards was my 38 days in a hell ship.

How did I survive? I have no answer. Stubbornness perhaps. Maybe just the determination to fulfill the promise that I made to myself when Corregidor fell that no Japanese was going to kill me. There was also a lot of luck. My ship wasn't bombed on the way to Japan. I got off Palawan before the massacre that wiped out my friends. I don't have an answer.

Tom Brokaw referred to us as "The Greatest Generation." I am not a hero. I joined the Marines to earn money to finish college. I had no wish to be heroic; I was being practical during the Depression. People call me a hero. I'm not. My country needed me, and I did my job. That's what Americans do.

I always stayed one step ahead of what could happen. My vow was that I would not be killed by the enemy and would one day be free. I kept that vow. I survived.

These are my suggestions for surviving:

Survival Top-Ten

1. **Food Survival**—Don't eat unwashed fruit! Coconuts, bananas, papayas, tree hearts, peppers, pineapples—ok.
2. **Incidences**—beer, be smarter than guards, dump truck; John Hughes—warned me on Palawan to listen to instinct
3. **Back to Bilibid**—became a landscaper because that was needed as laborers
4. **Back to Cabanatuan**—got myself transferred to Las Piñas
5. **Las Piñas**—outside work, could find food, had G-string and straw hat; tried to have camp currency—too much inflation, hoarding—had 10,000 pesos in G-string
6. **Desperation**—self-inflicted injuries—broke 14 arms—got caught when I broke a left-handed man's right arm
7. **Gratitude** — saved from trial at Las Piñas by US Navy bombings
8. **Hopelessness** — hell ship—up to fate
9. **Purgatory** — Mitsubishi mines, Northern Japan; waiting for end—release or execution
10. **Salvation**— American victory, Freedom

I swore that I would survive and would return to the United States and live a productive, full life. No one would take my future from me. I stayed one step ahead.

Afterword

A Descendant's Journey

"I don't consider myself a hero. My country needed me. I served. That's what Americans do."

George Burlage reflecting on his time as a prisoner-of-war

George Burlage passed away on November 30, 2008, at the age of ninety.

His daughter and many other POW descendants have traveled to the Philippines and to Japan to witness and experience their fathers' journeys. It is their generation's mission to honor their fathers' courage and sacrifices.

The legacy of the "Greatest Generation" endures, and the influence of this very special group continues. A quality witnessed in so many of this generation is humility. As George often said, "I didn't save anything or anybody. My country needed me, and I served."

This generation's sacrifice changed the world. They didn't claim to be heroes. They believed that they were only fulfilling their duty to their nation, and they more than succeeded. They fought, they sacrificed, and few ever questioned. We owe them so much.

—Georgianne Burlage

I doubt that when my father was liberated from Sendai #3 camp on September 2, 1945, he ever imagined that his future daughter would be at that camp almost seventy-four years to the day after his release. There I was, standing outside the mine entrance on September 4, 2019. Representatives from Mitsubishi Materials (the mine's owner) were waiting to welcome descendants of the prisoners-of-war who once worked as slave laborers there. I'm sure that our arrival and reception were far better than my dad's in January 1945.

I was in Japan as a participant in the United States-Japan POW Friendship Program. This program was started in 2010 by the Japanese government to invite former POWs to return to Japan with all expenses covered. Several POWs did return. But as age and death claimed more of the former prisoners, descendants began to participate. My group consisted of eight descendants, and three of us were visiting Sendai #3.

The Tokyo I visited was far different from the Tokyo that my dad passed through on his way to the mines. He described his arrival in the city in January 1945. The train station was constructed from wood, and the city was eerily quiet. The emaciated, filthy prisoners-of-war were an oddity in this Japanese city. Of course, the train station was a casualty of the fire bombings in the spring of 1945. The new train station is a huge maze and practically unnavigable without assistance.

It was from the megamouth train station that I boarded a bullet train to Sendai to visit my dad's former camp. The 225 miles between Tokyo and Sendai were completed in around ninety minutes, a contrast with the narrow-gauge railroad that George was on for this journey in 1945. He described that journey, explaining that with every mile traveled north, he became colder, and the train struggled to climb into the mountains. His pants were too short, leaving exposed legs. No Japanese pants were long enough to cover his more than six-foot height. He had lost almost half of his pre-war weight, but his height, of course, was the same.

After leaving our train at a smaller depot near the massive city of Sendai, we traveled by van into the mountain area. When the POWs arrived at this area in 1945, they were marched through the snow to the mine.

On the drive, I learned that representatives from Mitsubishi Materials were waiting for us at the mine. Mitsubishi is the only Japanese company that has apologized to POWs and their families for using slave labor during World War II. The other major companies—Mitsui, Nissan Steel, Showa Denko, and Kawasaki Heavy Industries—have yet to acknowledge their actions during the war. Mitsubishi also owned dockyards and coal mines and used slave labor in those industries. Their apology covered all use of slave labor, not just at the mines. Several lawsuits from former prisoners-of-war have been filed, but little has resulted. Japanese laws and the San Francisco Peace Treaty that ended World War II hostilities between Japan and the Allied nations make it very difficult to gain any reparations. My dad had long ago released his anger about his POW experiences, but he became very interested in these reparation lawsuits. He often stated that the Mitsubishi "triple diamonds" emblem still haunted him. I was shocked in the early 2005s when I was shopping for a new car, and my dad suggested looking at Mazdas and Hondas. "It's OK," he said. "I'm over it. However, no Nissans or Mitsubishis. Nissan used POW slave labor, and I don't want to see those damn triple diamonds in my garage." (Nissan was located in Manchuko, the Japanese Army's puppet state in Manchuria. They were one of the Japanese army's major truck suppliers.)

When my father was the regional public affairs officer for the Federal Aviation Administration's Southwestern Region, he was assigned to write a story about the Mitsubishi aircraft manufacturing plant in San Angelo, Texas. This was a story that he did not want to write, and my mother and I heard his complaints. He made the trip, interviewed Japanese officials, was photographed with several, and wrote the story for a FAA publication. He did share with us his feelings when he had to ride in a Mitsubishi car around the San Angelo area. We understood how he must have felt, but as a professional, he internalized his feelings, smiled, and admired the triple diamonds. And here I was, walking across a parking lot to shake hands with high-ranking officials of "those triple diamonds" near Sendai, Japan.

This was a moment that I never thought I would experience—I, the daughter of a World War II prisoner-of-war/slave laborer shaking the hand of a grandson of a World War II Japanese veteran and a representative of Mitsubishi in the front lot of the mine where my father worked. When I met the official, my sense of incredulity was expressed in my opening statement, "My dad was here." That's all I could think —my dad was here.

After formalities and a personal statement from Mitsubishi of regret of the treatment of the World War II POWs, we were shown the camp. There are a few original buildings remaining from the war era, and we met in one of those as a group. This mine closed in 1987 and now includes the Hosokura Mine Park. I stood at the entrance to the old mine and remembered the story of my dad being struck on the back with a board because he included profanities in the morning prayer before the Shinto shrine at the entrance. I asked about the road that the prisoners walked from their camp to the mine and was shown where it was. The road is still visible, but the camp is long gone. I could visualize the starving, cold prisoners making their ways down the path to work in what was becoming a never-ending war and captivity.

Mitsubishi displays a plaque by the former path of the POWs that states:

In Memory of WWII POWs

During World War II, military personnel of the Allied Forces captured by the Japanese military were forced to work in mines and factories throughout Japan. This included the Hosokura Branch of the Sendai POW camp that was under the control of the Japanese military and located at this site. In all, 281 POWs (234 Americans, 45 British, and one Dutch) were held at the camp at the end of the war. 19 POWs died in captivity.

Working conditions for the POWs were exceedingly harsh and left deep mental and physical wounds that the lapse of time would not heal.

POWs were subjected to similar conditions in the mines of Osarizawa (Akita Prefecture), Ikuno (Hyogo Prefecture) and Akenobe (Hyogo Prefecture), which were also operated by the former Mitsubishi Mining Company.

Reflecting on these tragic past events with the deepest sense of remorse, Mitsubishi Materials offers its heartfelt apologies to all former POWs who were forced to work under appalling conditions in the mines of the former Mitsubishi Mining Company and reaffirms its unswerving resolve to contribute to the creation of a world where fundamental human rights and justice are fully guaranteed.

November 2016 Mitsubishi Materials Corporation

The statement "Mitsubishi Materials offers its heartfelt apologies to all former POWs who were forced to work under appalling conditions in the mines" was the statement that my father waited more than sixty years to hear. Now, I could accept that apology for my dad.

From this mine camp, we visited one of the strangest amusement parks that I have seen. It is "Hosokura Mine Park," and there are rides, a gift shop, and access to the other part of the huge mine. The mine has been restored, and models of miners in various roles are displayed along with explanations. Unfortunately for Americans, the explanations are in Japanese. The entrance to the mine has a giant statue of the park mascot. The mascot wears a pink shirt with a giant "H" on the front. I could hear my dad saying, "What the hell is that?" Touring this part of the mine cave, I could understand how my father developed claustrophobia.

We left the mine park with the good wishes of the Mitsubishi officials. I talked with one of the men while walking to our van. He said that he again was sorry that my father was a slave laborer at the mine. My answer was sincere. "That was seventy-five years ago. He had a wonderful life, and the POW experience was a small part of his ninety years. Thank you for your kindness today."

He told me that his grandfather had been in World War II and added, "In the end, we are all one people." He was right. World War II is not our generations' fight. It is our legacy.

THE BEGINNING OF MY JOURNEY

My journey to share my father's World War II experiences began in April 2017 when I visited the Philippines. My day on Corregidor, where he was captured, coincidentally was his ninety-ninth birthday.

I had no idea what to expect on Corregidor. I really didn't know much about the place except that it was an island. During the ferry trip across Manila Bay to the island, I thought about my dad's experiences there seventy-five years earlier. All he really shared with me was that the armed forces didn't have enough ammunition, MacArthur abandoned them, there was a huge tunnel (Malinta Tunnel), and the final battle was short. We docked on the north side of the island, and I was amazed to see ruins of buildings. Corregidor had been a thriving, important military fortress for the United States-controlled Philippine Islands. The shell of the commissary, movie theater, the Mile-Long Barracks, and other buildings still stood. The battery areas were still there. It wasn't difficult to imagine the beleaguered Marines and soldiers rationing their inadequate weapons (my dad once told me that he had fifteen minutes' total worth of ammunition) and taking cover in the storage rooms. I recognized the bluff over the South China Sea from his descriptions, the bluff on which he ordered younger Marines to stand watch for relief ships that never came to boost morale.

Corregidor is quiet and populated by ghosts. I felt the presence of the men who served and who died, the men who fought and were captured, the hopelessness of the battle, and the finality of surrender.

Then I saw the 92nd Garage area, the small strip of beach where thousands of captive Americans and Filipinos were held in the tropical sun with no water, cover, or food. It was in this area that my dad stole a Japanese soldier's canteen and realized that if he just stayed aware and planned ahead, he could survive being a prisoner-of-war. It was on this beach that he swore that he would survive the war.

This beach area is covered in what are known as "blood rocks." These are rocks that turn red when the tide comes in, and the legend is that the color is a result of the blood that was spilled at Corregidor. I picked up a rock and threw it into the bay to honor my dad's birthday. I also took three of these rocks home—one for each of my daughters and one for me.

From Corregidor, I reversed my father's journey from Bataan to the island. We were placed in bancas, open Filipino boats, to be taken across the Bay of Bataan. There was no dock on the other side, and we had to depart our boats walking across ladders.

I also visited the sites of several POW camps where my dad had been held. His first POW prison was Bilibid City Jail in Manila. The original building still stands in one of the poorer areas of the city. Our guide told us to go in, take our photos, don't speak to anyone, and leave. It is a depressing place and is designed like a wheel with the spoke being the guard tower/offices and the cells extending from the spoke center. Nothing is left of Cabanatuan but the foundations of a few guard towers. I walked the perimeter and attempted to imagine the area as an area of death and suffering. This was the camp that my father asked to leave because of the rampant disease and starvation and subsequently was sent to Palawan.

At Subic Bay, the site of a former American Navy base, a large memorial overlooks the bay, honoring the prisoners-of-war who were placed aboard hell ships. The tour participants whose fathers were on a hell ship traveled aboard a ferry and sailed out into Subic Bay to lay a wreath in honor of our fathers' voyages. When we had arrived to board, we saw that the boat was anchored a few yards offshore and that we would have to wade out to get on. I hesitated at first and then said to myself, "Your father spent 38 days in the hold of a ship. Get with it."

Chance plays a major part in survival. Why in war are some ships bombed and others remain untouched? Why does a young man survive while his comrades die? How did some men survive the prisoner-of-war forced marches and labor and the hell ships, but others didn't? This question was on the minds of our self-named "Hell Ship Kids" as we sailed on the boat into the bay. Our mission was to honor our fathers who were aboard hell ships in World War II.

We were a trio who shared a bond of being the descendants of men who endured close to the worst that man can inflict on other men. Two of our dads survived the ordeal. One did not.

Our backgrounds were different. Margaret's dad survived the Bataan Death March. My dad had survived Corregidor. We had decades with our fathers after the war.

Joe's father, however, did not survive the war. His hell ship, the *Arisan Maru*, was attacked on October 24, 1944, by an American submarine. No POWs were killed by the torpedo, but only nine survived the ship sinking. The Japanese would not rescue any of the prisoners. The nine survivors reached China on one of the ship's lifeboats, and the story of the hell ships was finally known.

Joe never met his father because he was born during the Battle of Bataan. Charles Brown was serving with the US Army and was stationed in the Manila area when World War II began. He fought at Bataan, survived the death march, and was imprisoned in the Philippines in several camps including Cabanatuan where Margaret's and my dad served some time.

I met Joe and Margaret while on tour in the Philippines. We were waiting to board a boat to travel to Corregidor. After introductions, Joe opened his wallet and pulled out a small strip of metal to show me. It was inscribed "Daddy 3-4-43" on one side and "J. W. Brown" on the other.

This is Joe's only memento of his father. The metal strip was smuggled out of the camp by a Catholic priest who managed to give it to Joe's family. The priest was later captured and executed for his attempts to help POWs. Joe's mother was a Spanish citizen and was not placed in a civilian internment camp in Manila.

A week after the Corregidor visit, our tour visited the American Cemetery in Manila. Another new friend, Dino Armstrong, and I helped Joe locate his dad's name on the Missing-in-Action walls. Among the 39,000 names listed on those walls, we found Charles Brown.

After paying respects and taking photos, Joe told me he would help me find my dad's name. I looked at Joe and shook my head.

"I forgot," he said. "Your dad made it."

Yes, my dad did make it. He was among the estimated 60 percent of all POWs who did survive captivity. Why did he survive, and Joe's dad and thousands of others didn't? I guess it comes down to luck, just sheer luck. Why was Joe's dad on a doomed ship and my and Margaret's fathers weren't? Of course, there are no answers.

I know that George Burlage had survivors' guilt, especially about his friends at Palawan. George had a wonderful, successful post-World War II life. However, as his daughter, I know that he always wondered why he lived when so many did not.

He survived because he was always one step ahead— and, as he always maintained — he must have had a guardian angel. Some things just have no answer. Throughout my time in the Philippines, I often said to my father's spirit, "How did you survive this? How did you make it?"

My ten days in the Philippines ended at the American Cemetery in Manila. More than 36,000 names are engraved on the Tablets of the Missing walls at the cemetery. I was overcome by a great feeling of gratitude that George Burlage's name was not on that wall.

Many decades have passed since the end of World War II. Most of the participants are gone. Still, their presence is strong where they fought and suffered. My dad was with me on every step of my journey.

—Georgianne Burlage

Tributes to George Burlage

The Quiet Heroism of George Burlage

Originally published on December 4, 2008, in the Denton Record-Chronicle

It is impossible to accurately quantify the sacrifices made by individuals in time of war, but we think it would be safe to say that few men suffered more for their country than George Edward Burlage did during World War II.

Burlage, who enlisted in the Marines in 1939, was stationed in the Philippines when the war broke out and was captured by the Japanese in 1942 after the battle of Corregidor. He then spent more than three years as a slave laborer in the Philippines and in the Mitsubishi coal mines in Japan.

He was transported to Japan aboard one of the notorious "hell ships," in which American prisoners were crammed to overflowing into the darkened holds of cargo freighters for the voyage to the Japanese slave labor camps.

The holds were sealed shut with little or no food or water inside them. Many prisoners died or went mad on the voyages. One Japanese officer described the condition of one boatload of prisoners:

"Many men lost their minds and crawled about in absolute darkness armed with knives, attempting to kill people in order to drink their blood, or armed with canteens filled with urine and swinging them in the dark. The hold was so crowded, and everyone so interlocked with one another that the only movement possible was over the heads and bodies of others."

Ships were not marked as POW vessels, and so were frequently attacked by American airplanes and submarines. These aerial and torpedo attacks killed thousands of American prisoners.

Burlage survived the privations of the hell ships and the Japanese coal mines to be liberated in September 1945. He weighed 100 pounds when he was freed.

Burlage retired from the Marine Corps in 1959 and moved to Denton with his wife and family. Here he got a degree in journalism from what is now the University of North Texas and worked for a time as the regional editor of this newspaper.

He later worked for the Federal Aviation Administration as a regional public affairs officer until his retirement in 1983.

If Burlage's story of survival in wartime is remarkable – and it truly is – the story of his postwar years is just as remarkable, though in an entirely different way. The story of his wartime heroism was common knowledge around Denton, but not because of George Burlage. He never talked about it, never used his sacrifices for personal gain or aggrandizement. He simply settled into a life of public service— with the FAA, with virtually every veterans group in the area. He also worked to further the cause of education, endowing a scholarship at UNT for future teachers.

And he also— this is perhaps the most important thing he did— immersed himself in the simple glories of American family life. He was an avid gardener, once winning the Yard of the Month award from Keep Denton Beautiful, and a doting grandfather.

These things— his home, his family— were the things George Burlage fought for, and they were the things he prized— not the war stories or the recognition that came from his military service.

As a family man and a good citizen of Denton, Texas, that's just what he did until his death on Sunday at the age of 90. His quiet heroism reminds us yet again of the debt we owe the men and women of his generation. Remembering him is one way we repay that debt.

Tribute to George Burlage's Hell Ship Experiences

From **Corps Value: Everything You Need to Know I Learned in the Marines**

(copyright 1996, published by Longstreet Press, Marietta, Georgia)

by former Senator and Governor of Georgia, Zell Miller

Background: Zell Miller served as a Marine at Camp Lejeune, North Carolina, in the mid-1950s. His supervisor was Msgt. George Burlage.

Fifty years later, Sen. Miller reconnected with Burlage. Miller was exiting the Dallas-Fort Worth International Airport when he noticed the exit to Denton. He remembered that his former sergeant lived in Denton and looked him up. A friendship followed, and Burlage made several trips to Atlanta, Georgia, and later Washington, D. C., to visit with Senator Miller.

In 1998, Zell Miller dedicated Corps Values to his old sergeant and friend. He wrote that Msgt. George Burlage provided a postgraduate course in Corps Values at Camp Lejeune.

Miller described Burlage in his chapter entitled "Courage":

Now nearly 80, (George) Burlage, is as rough and tough as ever, reinforcing my belief that "Top" was indestructible and would continue in life as long as the Corps itself.

To Master Sergeant George Burlage, the prisoner of war experience was more than the graphic pages of some book— it was the personal experience which he had endured and miraculously survived during World War II.

"Top" had been out of Japanese prisons less than 10 years and had served another demanding tour of duty in Korea when I served under him.

He had been captured on Corregidor early in the war and spent three years in various Japanese prisoner of war camps in the Philippines and in Japan. He saw most of his comrades die, and he was subjected to beatings, torturous work details, and periods of starvation when no food was given to him for days. Since most POW experiences are too horrendous for those of us who have not gone through them to understand, I know he was inclined to understate them but, based on what I learned from his accounts, I always will hold in total awe and utmost admiration those who lived through such hellish ordeals.

(George) suffered from malaria, acute dysentery, beriberi, and pellagra and saw his weight dropped from 200 to 108 pounds. But he endured it for forty months and even lives through being stacked like cordwood with other prisoners in the hold of a ship and transported to Japan. He and the others had no food or water for days, and twenty to fifty men died each day, the weaker being so demented from thirst that they would try to bite open the throats of others for a drink of blood. The living lay side-by-side with the dead until the bodies were hauled out and dumped overboard.

Few live through that hell, and those who did so survived only because they had courage beyond belief.

Of all my heroes of all times, George Burlage is at the top of the list. Whenever I feel discouraged, disheartened, or weary, I make it a point to think of him and all that he survived and overcame, and I always feel renewed in body and spirit.

Thank Yous

During the thirty months spent editing and writing this book, many people have encouraged me. My daughters and sons-in-law Rachel Burlage and Marc Knight and Leah Burlage and Jerry Vela offered advice and proofreading. Thank you for helping in my project to share the story of your incredible grandfather.

Jeff Weil and Susan Horne also assisted with proofreading and background military information and maps. Thank you. Beth Bishop, Margaret Calabrese, and Andrea Hasse kept me writing and encouraged me, and Julie Tolle assisted with the final proofreading.

I also would like to thank my grandmother, Cora Rebecca ("Becky") Crawford Burlage. She passed away seven years before I was born, but she left me my father's World War II legacy. Becky Burlage saved every telegram, letter, photo, and newspaper article about her prisoner-of-war son. I cannot begin to imagine the heartache and worry that she endured during the forty months that her son was a captive. Without her vision to keep these items, hoping that George would return home to see these himself, we would not have a complete record of his World War II service and imprisonment.

This book would not have been possible without the members of the "Greatest Generation" who literally saved the world. This unassuming group left the United States to fight for our freedoms in places that few Americans had ever heard of and when they returned, they truly lived the American Dream that they had protected. I doubt if we will ever see a generation this brave and humble again.

I am also grateful for my father George Burlage who not only served his country but wrote hundreds of pages about what he experienced. I am still discovering notes that he wrote. When I was working on revisions for this book, I found a scrap of paper in a book about General MacArthur where he had written comments about the hell ship experience. He wrote when inspired, and he wrote on legal pads, envelopes, and shopping lists and typed volumes. My dad obviously had a story to share, and this is what this book accomplishes. My hope is that his story will inspire, educate, and make us realize how fortunate we are to have had this generation serve our nation.

Georgianne Burlage/Denton, Texas/November 2019

Background Information on POWs

Most prisoners-of-war of the Japanese spent almost the entirety of World War II in captivity. Most of these prisoners were captured in the spring of 1942 in the Philippines, Indochina, and the Dutch East Indies.

A total of 36,230 American military were POWs. 14,000 American civilians who were living in areas occupied by the Imperial Japanese government were also put in POW camps including men, women, and children.

Forty percent of American POWs held by Japan died in captivity. Many of these were killed aboard hell ships when attacked by American bombers. These prisoners were being transported from the Philippines to slave labor camps in occupied areas and Japan. One percent of Americans held by the Germans died as POWs.

Ninety percent of POWs in World War II who died in captivity were held by the Japanese.

25,000 American POWs were sent to be slave laborers of large Japanese corporations. Mitsui, Mitsubishi, Showa Denko, Nippon Steel, and Kawasaki Heavy Industries were the largest users of POW slave labor. In total, more than forty industries used slave labor. Only Mitsubishi has apologized to the former POWs and their families. Thousands of POWs were used to build the Burma-Siam Railway.

55.279 Allied POWs were put on hellships to be sent to slave labor camps. 10,853 POWs drowned due to American attacks on the convoys (3,622 Americans were killed aboard hellships). Approximately 500 died of disease, thirst, and starvation aboard these ships.

At the end of the war, 12,180 American POWs were working as slave laborers in Japan.

Information from U.S. Department of Veterans Affairs website

Bibliography

n.d. *4th Marine Regiment: The Oldest and the Finest.* Accessed January 25, 2020. https://www.3rdmardiv.marines.mil/Units/4th-Marine-Regiment/History/.

Brady, James. 2003. *Flyboys: A True Story of Courage.* Boston, MA: Little, Brown, and Company.

Center of Military History, United States Army. 1989. *The War in the Pacific- The Fall of the Pilippines.* Washington D.C.: United States Army.

n.d. *Corregidor.og/usmc.* Accessed December 29, 2019. www.corregidor.org/usmc/chs_41-42/marines.htm.

Davis, Gavan. 1994. *Prisoners of the Japanese: POWs of World War II in the Pacific.* New York: Quill William Morrow.

Flanagan, Damian. 2016. *Japanese Times.* July 23. Accessed December 29, 2019. japanesetimes.co.jp.

Gordon, John. 2011. *Fighting for MacArthur: The Navy and Marine Corps' Desperate Defense of the Phillipines.* Annapolis: Naval Institute Press.

Lord Russell of Liverpool, CBE, MC. 2002. *The Knights of Bushido: A Short History of Japanese War Crimes.* London: Greenhill Books.

MacArthur, Brian. 2005. *Surviving the Sword: Prisoners of the japanese in the Far East 1942-45.* New York: Random House .

n.d. *Mansell.com.* Accessed December 29, 2019. www.mansell.com.

Michno, Gregory F. 2001. *Death on the Hellships: Prisoners at Sea During the Pacific War.* Annapolis, MD: Naval Institute Press.

Miller, J. Michael. 1997. *From Shanghai to Corrgidor: Marines in the Defense of the Philippines.* Washington, D.C.: Marine Corps Historical Center.

n.d. *PTSD: National Center for PTSD.* Accessed December 28, 2019. www.ptsd.va.gov.

Shaw, Frank. n.d. *Victory and Occupation: History of the US Marine Corps Operations in World War II.* Accessed January 29, 2020. https://www.ibiblio.org/hyperwar/USMC/V/USMC-V-A.html.

Index